Teaching the Disorderly Pupil

By the same authors:

Practical School Discipline and Mental Hygiene
Better Home Discipline
Bright Children
The Only Child
Teaching the Bright and Gifted

TEACHING THE DISORDERLY PUPIL

in Elementary and Secondary School

NORMA E. CUTTS, Ph.D.

Professor of Psychology and Education
Southern Connecticut State College

and

NICHOLAS MOSELEY, Ph.D.

Educational Consultant

DAVID McKAY COMPANY, INC.

New York

Teaching the Disorderly Pupil

Copyright . 1957

by

David McKay Company, Inc.

Published simultaneously in the Dominion of Canada

First Edition July 1957
Reprinted February 1959
September 1962

Library of Congress Catalog Card Number 57-12119

Printed in the United States of America

Contents

Contents

Foreword

There was a time, not so long ago, when teachers were afraid to say that classroom discipline was a problem. Any such admission was looked on as a confession of weakness. This attitude is rapidly changing, if, indeed, it has not altogether changed.

Teachers today recognize that misbehavior in school is most often a sign of maladjustment. The pupil who will not cooperate with his classmates and with the teacher is generally faced with some difficulty he has not been able to overcome. This difficulty may be in his home situation, it may be a physical or mental disability, or it may be in the school situation itself. The teacher, instead of blaming himself as a poor disciplinarian or the pupil as incorrigible, is challenged to find the cause of the pupil's misbehavior and to help him to adjust.

But a pupil who continually misbehaves is a serious drain on the teacher's time and energy, an unpleasant element in the life of the classroom, and a definite drag on the work of other pupils. When a large number of pupils in one room are behavior problems, the burden is almost unbearable.

Whether the problem is one unruly kindergartner or a roomful of sullen, impertinent teen-agers, the teacher wants to know not only how to maintain or regain control and prevent disorder, but also how to help individuals and groups learn self-discipline and achieve good adjustment and good morale.

This book has been planned to give classroom teachers in both secondary and elementary schools an understanding of the common causes of classroom misbehavior. It describes methods that successful teachers use to control and prevent misbehavior while working to help the pupil adjust. And it includes specific suggestions that teachers can pass on to the others most concerned: parents, pastors, recreation leaders, and, most particularly, the pupil himself. In the belief that teachers can and should be community leaders or at least active in community affairs, we try to point out ways in which, as members of committees or as individuals, they can combat common conditions that are largely responsible, first, for disorder in the classroom, and later, for delinquency, mental illness, and social maladjustment. In line with this policy we have placed at the end of each chapter except the first a selection of books and pamphlets worth reading, a list of topics for study and research, a list of community and school projects worth working for, and suggestions for films and topics for a PTA meeting. To lead groups of parents to consider problems related to discipline is a particularly valuable service because so much maladjustment originates in the home.

The suggestions we make are based on materials contributed in 1955-57 by more than five hundred teachers and more than one thousand students as well as upon our own experience in teaching and administration and in work with maladjusted children. The quotations that open each chapter are from our materials. Because we promised anonymity we cannot make personal acknowledgments, but we are grateful to the teachers and pupils who contributed.

The book does not offer any magic cure-all. Teaching, especially in these days of large classes, crowded buildings, and long hours, is hard work. Discipline is an integral part of the job. When the teacher's efforts bring improvement, not only in the tone of the classroom but most especially in the individual pupil's adjustment to life, the teacher knows a reward that makes the work light.

Teaching the Disorderly Pupil

I

The Problem of Discipline

. . . the problem of "increased restlessness in the classroom," "discipline in the classroom" and "general school discipline."
> —Report of the Commission on Defense of the Public Schools, National Education Association, July 21, 1955.

Looking at myself and my fellow students from a teacher's point of view, I think I would end up in a madhouse if I were one.

The abuses range from disobedience to violence.

The teachers are not strict enough! Are they afraid of the children? Or are they afraid of the administration? I don't know. But I couldn't stand that.
> —Excerpts from high-school students' comments on teaching as a career.

A child, known as the group leader . . . is responsible for maintaining discipline—that is, for seeing that the ordinary rules of courtesy are observed.
> —Dorothy Norris, "Special Classes for the Gifted in Cleveland, Ohio."

However you yourself define discipline, and whether you use the word as a verb or a noun, you probably have no doubt what is meant whenever teachers use the phrase, "the problem of discipline." The central thought is always that of order. There may be differences of opinion about the best methods of achieving good order or even about what good order is, but there is unanimity of feeling that where disorder is the rule of the day a problem exists and better discipline is desirable.

DEGREES OF DISORDER

For twenty years now we have been collecting, from teachers, pupils, parents, psychologists, the press, and the professional literature, accounts of what children do that teachers think they should not do and what actions teachers take to correct misbehavior. Amongst our materials are two sets of diaries kept by teachers, one set in 1937 and one in 1955. In each year, several teachers wrote down, hour by hour and day by

day, brief anecdotes of every bit of behavior they corrected—
or deliberately ignored. They also furnished more detailed accounts of the backgrounds of chronic offenders (children who
kept appearing in the diaries) and of their own long-range
plans for securing a basic change in these children's attitudes.

The diarists generally treat the misdemeanors of pupils
with good-humored tolerance. These teachers are not martinets
or scolds. But they find it necessary to exercise a great deal of
what we call "simple control" to stop undue talking, restless
moving, and attacks on others. Often such control takes the
form of a smile or a word or a question that the alert teacher
directs at a child who is about to forget himself. (As one high-
school student said, "He knows what we're going to do before
we do.") Practically all these teachers resort on occasion to
some form of punishment. Even the best say they sometimes
get cross. But all of this—today as when we were in school
and when our parents were in school—is almost automatic.
The teacher is surprised when he reads his notes to see
how often he has corrected behavior. The children, if they
think about it at all, say, "He was right," or, "I deserved it,"
and, with youthful optimism, "I won't do that again."

The problem of discipline does not lie in the semiautomatic
correction of casual misbehavior, but in the difficulty of dealing with chronic offenders. These are the pupils who, despite
all the teacher can do, are constantly disturbing the class.
Younger children of this sort are reported as always fighting
or pushing other children. They are never in their seats. They
continually talk out of turn and interrupt the teacher and the
other children. The older chronic offender is not above fighting
or pushing, and he, too, is given to talking at the wrong time.
He is also likely to fail regularly in many aspects of schoolwork, to ignore or directly disobey directions or to be deliberately impertinent when he is spoken to, to break school
regulations, and to be truant or cut classes frequently. At all
grade levels, boys outnumber girls among the chronic offenders
by 7 to 1. (This is, perhaps significantly, almost exactly the
proportion of males to females among adults arrested for
major crimes.)

The majority of the class usually disapprove the things the
chronic offenders do, though most boys and girls will sometimes make a teacher's life miserable by following a bad
example or stopping work to form an appreciative audience
for the bear-baiter. But neither group pressure nor any form of
official punishment seems to change the chronic offender's
behavior for the better. More often, continued disapproval and
punishment make matters worse.

IS THE PROBLEM INCREASING?

Almost every teacher has in his class one or more pupils whom he finds some difficulty in controlling. Elementary-school teachers are divided on whether or not discipline is more difficult today than it used to be. One remarks acutely, "I certainly feel that some of the problems I face are more serious than any I used to have, but this may be because I'm more aware of the implications. I know more than I did about how emotional maladjustment originates and about how hard it is to overcome."

Secondary-school teachers are practically unanimous in their opinion that discipline is more of a problem today than it ever was, and that the problem grows more burdensome every year. We have numerous accounts of high-school teachers who are leaving to enter other kinds of work, who are trying to transfer to other school positions—for example, in the guidance department—which will relieve them of responsibility for regular classes, or who are retiring the minute they qualify for their pensions though this means a considerable financial sacrifice. One 50-year-old mathematics teacher, who has just retired on a minimum pension, writes: "I felt guilty when the superintendent begged me to stay. I know how hard math teachers are to get. I agree that I owe the system a debt of loyalty after thirty years. But I just can't take it any more. I'm sorry. But I really can't."

A committee of New York City high-school principals, meeting with their board of education, said, "We are shocked and depressed by the general failure of the authorities to understand the sorry deterioration in our high schools . . . . They are not the high schools of the good old days." The committee presented a bill of particulars, which included the statements: "Morale is at a record low. More insolence and indignities are being perpetrated than ever before. Delinquent children are being sent back to the schools because there are no correctional facilities available for them. High schools are receiving virtual nonreaders from the lower schools."

THE CAUSES OF MISBEHAVIOR

Our materials confirm the conclusion that all researchers into the problem of discipline have reached: The pupil who is habitually disorderly in school and defies standard measures of correction is a child with an unsolved personal problem or problems. Ill health or a physical handicap may interfere with his learning and cause aggressive behavior that is beyond his control. Low intelligence or a subject-matter disability may make it impossible for him to follow the standard curriculum: the "virtual nonreader" in Grade X is more fitted to exemplify Caliban than to study The Tempest. The home environment is frequently at the root of his difficulty. Many boys and girls who are chronic offenders come from homes broken by divorce, desertion, or death, or cracked by parental disharmony. Many are subject to one or several of the following conditions: a parent who is chronically ill, mentally ill, a drunkard, a prostitute, or a criminal; spoiling or discipline that is overstrict or inconsistent; faulty care due to lack of interest, lack of time, or outright rejection; a slum neighborhood lacking in facilities for wholesome recreation but replete with warring gangs.

These conditions place a child under strains that may cause maladjustment. They interfere with the normal satisfaction of his need for love, security, and recognition. He is, in the old phrase, a "neglected child." His reaction is likely to be a strenuous attempt to call attention to himself. Because misbehavior is rarely ignored either at home or at school, he regularly misbehaves. But his misbehavior, though it secures undoubted recognition, brings him neither love nor security, but rather the opposite. His frustration results in continued aggressive misbehavior or, more dangerously, in withdrawal into a world of fantasy.

Practically every classroom has some children affected by one or more of the handicaps we have been discussing, and, thus, some children who are inclined to serious misbehavior. The statistics show that if you teach 30 pupils in a school in Middletown, U.S.A., the chances are that 2 or more will come from homes broken by divorce or desertion, and 1 or more will have a parent who is or has been mentally ill. The kind of neighborhood in which your school is located determines, of course, how many of your pupils are subject to the evil influences of slums, and to some extent how many of your pupils have parents with criminal records. But our materials contain tragic cases of children from good neighborhoods whose bad school behavior started with the arrest of a parent. And there are many alcoholic adults at every social level. Considering the prevalence of distress in the world, it is astonishing that more children do not succumb. That they do not is to a considerable extent due to the efforts of skilled teachers.

THE CHALLENGE

Although the pupils who give you most trouble generally suffer from one or more of the difficulties we have mentioned, you will discover that other children who carry burdens as great or greater are among your most friendly, hard-working, likable youngsters. Some of our greatest men, including Abraham Lincoln and, more recently, Mr. Justice Cardozo, started life under the most difficult circumstances. Many living governors, corporation presidents, scientists, lawyers, and teachers were born in the slums, or grew up in broken homes, or were born physically handicapped. Many good, solid citizens have bad backgrounds and low IQ's as well. Moreover, many people who have been institutionalized for serious maladjustment recover fully and lead useful, normal lives.

If some children can thrive under the worst conditions, if some who fall can rise again and grow strong, we ought to be able to prevent mental and moral breakdowns in the great majority of cases. This is our hope and our challenge.

The challenge is direct to you, the teacher. You and your colleagues are the only representatives of the state who have firsthand continuing contact with all children. You are in a position to sense incipient difficulties. You can by yourself satisfy many of the emotional needs of children who, if these needs go unsatisfied, will become maladjusted. You can rally the help of school officials and other public and private agencies to diagnose and try to correct or compensate for the causes of misbehavior.

II

The Teacher and the Group

I have great admiration for anyone who can handle a group like this.
—Richard Nixon to his daughter's teacher,
Grade II.

Actually, Al is not a terrific behavior problem, but he is a constant nuisance and often starts everyone else off on a talking spree which disrupts the class.
—A teacher, Grade III.

Thank heaven, I have no other pupil with Bruce's trouble, but I do have more behavior problems in the class and they are more difficult to control because of Bruce's antics.
—A teacher, Grade VI.

A meek little teacher who "loves dear little children" should not instruct or be expected to discipline a bunch of rowdies.
—A high-school student.

If a pupil respects a teacher then he is more likely to behave. One of our teachers can walk into a room and say quietly, "That will be all, class," and everyone is quiet. Another teacher walks into class and hollers at us to be quiet, but the kids won't quiet down.
—A high-school student.

I worked very hard for them and soon they began to work for me.
—Admiral Sims.

Good morale in each classroom and in the whole school is the first essential of good discipline. If the emotional tone of the classroom is one of warm friendliness, pride in a good reputation, and group solidarity, every student means to do well. Even the maladjusted child, whose aggressive inclinations are generally beyond his control, tries his best to conform. And he may find in the attitude of the group the support he needs to succeed. But if teacher and pupils are antagonistic or if they are uncertain or afraid, a minor incident may set off a chain reaction.

Three kinds of teachers are likely to have trouble with discipline in any grade: the new, untried teacher; the experienced teacher who changes from a school where informality is the rule to a school full of rowdies who are accustomed to being governed with an iron rod; and the teacher who, because he is ill or old or bored or worried by family problems, no longer has any zest for his work. Furthermore, substitutes seem fair game in any school that has not good traditions of order and courtesy. In each of these cases the teacher is insecure or antagonistic, or both. And both insecurity and antagonism increase rapidly if a class gets out of hand and continues to be disorderly.

THE ROLE OF THE ADMINISTRATION

If you are nervous about starting in a new position or if you are having trouble with discipline, you wonder what help you have a right to expect from the principal or, in a big school, from other officials. The following brief outline of the role of the administration is based on the practice of a large number of successful principals of all kinds of schools. You should certainly feel free to ask for help along any of the lines indicated here—and, indeed, in any situation that is bothering you.

The atmosphere of a school is to a very large extent controlled by the principal. The good principal is a warm, courteous, friendly person who knows his job and likes his work. Teachers and pupils imitate him. He knows the strengths and weaknesses of each teacher and takes them into account when he is assigning pupils. He knows who the troublemakers among the students are, and manipulates his assignments so that gangs of troublemakers are broken up. He assists and coordinates the efforts of teachers, parents, and social workers to discover and remedy the causes of pupils' difficulties. When necessary, he sees to it that these efforts are carried on from year to year with as little lost motion as possible. He is aware of specific conditions in the building that may incite to misbehavior—crowded corridors and stairways, a room that is difficult to ventilate, a toilet wall that is easily marked with pencil—and works with the students to secure their cooperation in managing themselves under such conditions, the while he works with his superiors to remedy matters.

The good principal is democratic in his methods of promoting discipline in the school. He knows that a great deal could go on in his school of which he would never be aware unless teachers and students felt free to call his attention to problems and to make suggestions for changes. He talks over discipline in teachers' meetings and with groups of students, and makes all hands feel responsible for seeing that discipline is good. He does not confine the topic of discipline to a single, beginning-of-the-year meeting or consider it a question to be broached only in a crisis. Rather, he discusses discipline periodically, and puts the emphasis not on misdemeanors but on what each and every person can do to keep the school functioning smoothly and to keep morale at a high level.

The new teacher is a major responsibility of the principal. The theory that every teacher has to prove himself, has to learn to swim by risking the chance of drowning, results in a great many tragedies. The good principal makes it clear that he stands ready to back the teacher up. He lets the teacher know that there is no disgrace in sending a recalcitrant pupil to the office or in calling for help. He makes sure that the teacher knows what types of punishment may be employed with his full approval, so that the teacher is not caught in the predicament of one mentioned in a pupil's report: "Two boys started a fight, and the teacher, new to the school, didn't know what to do and just let the boys go." Another report on the same incident concludes, "And after that, didn't we give him a rough time."

Principals should try to give new teachers a visiting day early in the year, and perhaps arrange for a teachers' meeting to discuss their reports of what they have seen. Both the visit and the discussion help the inexperienced teacher realize that his problems are neither unique nor insuperable. One high-school sophomore writes: "I think if some of our teachers would go to a different school and see how kids are punished they would probably get a little more strict and the kids wouldn't fool around so much and would grow up to be better citizens."

The principal and the older teachers in the building should make plans to help inexperienced teachers through the first days and weeks of school. The opening of school is a busy time, but the principal should try to drop into each newcomer's room several times a day. If the principal cannot arrange to do this, he should ask a teacher whom the pupils know and like to do it for him. If someone visits a new teacher's class briefly but frequently, and if this is done for all new teachers, both the class and the teacher take it as a matter of course; there is then no feeling that anyone is spying on the teacher or thinks he is weak. Rather, the teacher gains in security because he feels the principal is interested in his work and ready to back him up.

THE PERSONALITY OF THE TEACHER

The characteristics of the good teacher have been described by many authors, including Geoffrey Chaucer, Henry Adams, and the writer of the latest novel about a beloved classroom martinet. And many professional educators have analyzed the qualities they find in successful teachers. There is general agreement that the good teacher likes young people, likes to teach, and is enthusiastic about his subject. Enthusiasm and humor are the traits most lauded, with objectivity, flexibility, and loyalty receiving honorable mention. Students, writing of what they like and dislike in teachers, fill in the details. They say that the good teacher is friendly and treats pupils like human beings—"He calls you by name when he meets you on the street." He is fair—"He always listens to both sides of the story." He is approachable and unhurried—"He takes time to talk to you." He has a sense of humor—"He's the first to see a joke." He is generally cheerful—"He doesn't get mad unless you make him." He has high standards and expects the class to live up to them—"He has gained the highest respect of the students by his strict manner of discipline along with his splendid sense of humor." He never bluffs—"He said, 'Well, I don't know the answer to that one, but I think we can find out.'" He dresses well and is well groomed—"She wears a new dress every day." He has a pleasant voice and a good enunciation—"You can always hear everything he says, and he never shouts." He has good health and high vitality—"He's full of pep."

Students criticize the teacher who is mean, scolds, nags, plays favorites, is sarcastic, too easygoing, or too strict. They are particularly hard on unpleasant mannerisms—"He's always picking his nose with a pencil."

Psychologists and psychiatrists believe that the traits that supervisors and students prefer in teachers are most likely to be present when the teacher is a well-adjusted person whose emotional needs are satisfied. Deep-seated anxiety and hostility make a poor teacher. Good courses in mental hygiene have helped many teachers to a better personal adjustment and have made them happier, more efficient teachers. It's important that such a course be given by an instructor who understands the difficulties teachers face in the classroom and who sympathizes with the teachers' point of view. Psychiatrists who have given such courses are themselves emphatic in this conclusion.

Probably the best advice anyone can give you on cultivating a good teaching personality is the simplest: be yourself. You can learn much from watching good teachers, but you cannot solve your difficulties merely by imitating some teacher that you like and admire. Unless you happen to be the same sort of person, you'll be as self-conscious as anyone else who poses before an audience, and your pupils will be quick to note that you are not genuine. A sophomore writes of a teacher that the class thought

fussy: "The reason she is trying to be strict is known by most
of the pupils––that she is trying to act like a certain other
woman teacher in our school." The criticism is aimed not at
strictness (the student's paper shows that he admires strictness), but at the aping of another's ways. So, be yourself!

BEFORE SCHOOL STARTS

If you can get off to a good start with a class, you minimize
the probability of group disorder and you put yourself in a
strategic position to handle the occasional chronic offender.
Communities, schools, and classes within a school are as subject to individual differences as are the pupils in a class. The
more you can know ahead of time about the specific situation in
which you will find yourself, the better. Even the experienced
teacher who has been teaching in the same school for several
years profits from careful study of a new class before he meets
them. For the beginning teacher and the teacher new to a district, detailed advance planning is practically essential. The
notes that follow here suggest some of the things you should try
to do. You may think the amount of work involved is un-
necessary. But if you will examine the suggestions carefully,
we think you will find that each concerns something that must be
done sooner or later. If you can do most or all of these things
before school closes in June, or even just before school opens
in September, you will gain security and be able to welcome
your new class with self-confidence.

Walk through the streets of the school district. Note cul-
tural and economic levels, recreational facilities, prevalent
religions and races.

Read the local newspapers.

Make an appointment with the principal and visit the school.
If he has time, ask him to talk with you about the curriculum,
methods, and discipline. Ask if he knows whether your class
will contain any unusual pupils, either good or bad. Ask him to
show you over the building. Make note of the building's resources: library, auditorium, nurse's room, playground. Locate
the toilets, drinking fountains, teachers' room. Meet the custodian.

Study your own room. Consider the furniture with a view to
possible arrangements for opening day, group work, plays, exhibits. Keep ease of circulation, access to cupboards, and
safety in mind. Are there desks and chairs for unusually tall
and short pupils? How are lighting, heat, and ventilation controlled?

Study the official curriculum and texts for your own grade and for those immediately above and below yours.

Study the cumulative records with a view to starting each pupil within the range of his achievement and ability. If the records contain notes on troublemakers, study them very carefully. If possible, talk with the last teacher of the class you are to have and ask his advice about how to handle individuals— and their parents.

Think out what you expect to do about seating. If the records mention children who are hard of hearing or visually handicapped, plan to seat them where they can hear and see most easily. Plan to keep known troublemakers separated. If you have no knowledge of handicapped children or troublemakers, you can tell the children when they come in on the first day to sit wherever they wish. You can rearrange them later, if it seems wise.

Memorize your class lists. If you are a high-school teacher with a hundred and fifty or more students, this may seem a chore. But remember that you will have to learn all the names before long. If you know them ahead of time, you soon put names and faces together. The students respect you for the feat. And the troublemaker is deprived of anonymity.

Prepare meticulously for the first day and week of school. Have ready more than you can possibly cover. Include some novel materials that you can use if you have special need to catch and hold the class's attention—a story to read, a game to play, a competitive type of drill.

THE FIRST DAY OF SCHOOL

Make your room and yourself as attractive as you can for the opening session. Dress well, but conservatively. (One new teacher started a wolf-whistle riot in a class of high-school boys by the sweater she wore on her first day.) Fill the bulletin board with current clippings. Put interesting books and magazines on the library table. Bring a vase or two full of autumn flowers. The idea is not to have everything complete and final and unmovable for the year, but rather to set the stage in a way that will make the pupils want to take part in the show.

Before the pupils arrive, it's a good idea to print your name and address on the board. If you are a secondary-school teacher and have office hours or make-up periods, list the times and place. Try to greet as many of the pupils individually as you can. Ask early arrivals their names (here you will begin to appreciate having memorized the lists and studied the records), introduce yourself, and call attention to the books and magazines on the library table.

Beginning with written work is one good way to help the class settle down. Have paper and pencils ready on the desks. Tell each pupil to put his full name, age, and address at the top of each sheet. This gives you a check on the records, and, if you circulate through the room as the pupils write, you can put many names and faces together. Some schools make a practice of having each pupil fill out a form that brings the permanent record up to date. If this isn't necessary, assign a topic that will give you a starting point for the opening discussion. Teachers of high-school subjects often ask the students to state what they expect to accomplish in the course and how they expect to use it after graduation. Teachers in all grades may find it interesting to ask the pupils to propose rules and methods for the efficient management of the room and the schedule. Other useful topics are: "What I Like Most in School," "What I Like Most Out of School," "What I Hope to Be," and, "What I Did in My Vacation."

Opinions of both teachers and students differ on whether it is best to have an immediate discussion of order and of the rules you want observed. We think it is a good idea, especially for an inexperienced teacher, provided that you are determined to enforce a rule that is once agreed upon, and provided you will keep the discussion friendly and base it upon reason. If you lay down the law, especially if you do it with an unpleasant, hostile manner, you're making trouble for yourself. One student writes: "Teachers should put it to students' faces that they are here to learn and to make something of themselves and if they don't want to learn they should get out." But another writes: "Some teachers will lay down the law from the beginning; this is especially true of new teachers. Usually they have had little experience with teen-agers and are simply ignored. To improve this, teachers should have more knowledge of students' feelings, likes, and dislikes. Maybe something has been left out of their education."

The way to avoid arbitrariness is to state the reason why some agreement is necessary about talking, moving around, or passing through the halls. Then you can either ask for suggestions or say pleasantly what you think should be done. If you use the latter approach, be sure to give the class a chance to discuss your ideas. Do not give the class a choice between alternatives unless you mean to accept their decision. If the class is drawing up rules, take a part in the discussion. If left entirely to themselves, the class will probably try to cover everything by rule, and they'll probably want to attach specific punishments for infractions of each rule. Both are mistakes.

Sometime soon after the year starts, perhaps even at the end of the first period in high school or the first day in elementary

school, you and the class should have an evaluation session on
how well the rules are being observed, whether or not any can
be eliminated, and whether any new rules are necessary.
Similar sessions can be held whenever an unforeseen situation
develops, for example, if crowding around lockers results in
a lot of pushing. And, from time to time during the year, you
will be wise to hold class discussions of discipline and morale.

FIRM AND FRIENDLY

The experience of generations of teachers backs the wisdom
of starting with a firm hand. Unfortunately, the emphasis on
democratic procedures in the classroom has been misunderstood by a great many students in education courses. They have
been led to believe that, if the teacher's methods are modern
enough, there will be no tendency to disorder on the part of
the class. The future teacher, with a natural abhorrence of becoming like the sour schoolmarm of the cartoon, looks forward
to a classroom where pupils work hard because they like the
teacher and because they wish to learn. But graduates in their
first year of teaching report that their greatest problems
center around "how to control the class," "how much freedom
to allow," and "general disorder." Their principals and supervisors confirm this situation.

There are many reasons for a tendency to disorder. Misbehavior in school is an exciting departure from the normal.
When pupils are accustomed to strict control in the home and
in other classrooms, the chance to break out releases stored-
up feelings of frustration. Defiance of a teacher and of set
standards caters to the need of growing children for independence and gives them a sense of power. If the teacher obviously suffers when he cannot restore order, continued disorder
appeals to that primitive sense of humor which enjoys
cruelty—a type of humor that many children have not out-
grown. The boldest misbehavior gains the most attention, and
so the pupils try to outdo each other. The class quickly becomes an unruly mob.

Students themselves have no doubt that the only way for a
teacher to avoid having unruly classes is to be firm and consistent in discipline from the beginning. The quotations that
follow are from 119 papers written by high-school students on
the topic, "Discipline in Our School." We believe that younger
pupils would agree with the comments.

There are a few classes where teachers take a beating so to speak. The
reason for this is he is not strict enough when first starting, and therefore the

kids in the lower grades know about this, and when they have this teacher they think he will be a breeze and start fooling around. I have had this teacher for three years, and I don't think it is fair.

I know that when a new young teacher comes in, if he doesn't show us who is boss right away, we give him the works.

I know myself what teachers let me get away with talking and fooling around.

Some slack teachers allow misbehavior to go unpunished. They give detention and get talked out of it. Believe me, if at first you don't succeed, don't try again. Respect is lost for these teachers, and students only laugh at them.

More than one-third of these students stated that teachers should be more strict. The strict teacher is, they think, more efficient.

If in study halls as well as classrooms, discipline was exercised more freely, maybe we'd get more studying done.

When two boys are fighting and some are throwing paper airplanes at the teacher and so on, it's pretty hard to study.

When kids come in and throw your books on the floor and won't admit it, it can be an awfully long day.

There is no reason, according to these students, why a teacher should not be strict and at the same time friendly and informal.

The best-liked teacher is strict but still nice at the same time.

I think the discipline would be improved a great deal if the teacher would: (a) be willing to laugh at something funny that happens in the classroom once in a while; and (b) let the students know who is boss in the classroom in any situation.

If a teacher is constant in his discipline, the students get accustomed to this and behave without question. Some teachers are very good about this and the students appreciate them for it, because they can enjoy an informal atmosphere in the class which puts everyone at their ease.

Our advice, then, is not to tolerate disorder in the classroom. The first challenge will probably come in the form of clowning, intentional misinterpretation of directions, or ostentatious disobedience. Know your powers and be ready to use them. Do not make any threats. Keep alert. Pounce on the first deliberate offender. Inflict a real but fair penalty. Strangely enough, if you are determined to follow this procedure, you may never have to do so.

We do not wish to exaggerate the problem of group disorder. The National Education Association survey, Teacher Opinion on Pupil Behavior, 1955-56, reported that more than 60% of the 4,270 teachers questioned stated that less than 1% of their pupils were troublemakers. Moreover, 38% of the elementary-school teachers, 12% of the junior-high-school teachers, and 16.7% of the senior-high-school teachers felt that they had no troublemakers in their classes. And when we ask pupils, "What is the last thing you did in your last school which your teacher thought you shouldn't have done?" many answer with one word, "Nothing." A seventh-grader elaborates: "I enjoyed everything I did. The teacher asked if we liked what we were doing and let us make a few suggestions of what we would like to do. I felt it was a good idea, what the teacher did."

AN OUNCE OF PREVENTION

Day by day and year by year you can keep your classroom a happy place to work and save yourself an infinite amount of unpleasantness if you will do all you can to prevent disciplinary difficulties. Prevention is a combination of knowing the tricks of the trade and of giving constant thought to how you can best serve each pupil in your classes. And to anyone who scorns tricks of the trade, we should like to point out that those we recommend require consideration for the individual, worthy objectives, and a high degree of professional skill.

Principals tell new teachers that the way to keep pupils in order is to keep them busy and interested. There is no better rule, if the activities in which the pupils are interested are intrinsically worth while. The use of mere "busywork" is but one degree more desirable than disorder. Perhaps we should state the rule in another way: "Be sure that your pupils have worth-while goals, immediate, intermediate, and long-range. A boy or girl or class interested in accomplishing a purpose has no inclination to waste time."

You can't expect a pupil in any grade to be interested in his work if it's too hard or too easy for him. The wide spread of ability in every class means that if you try to teach every pupil the same thing at the same time you are sure to go over the heads of some and to bore others. In fact, you bore both. A high-school sophomore writes, "Some teachers expect the students to be smarter than they are and they talk about things far above their heads, so the students have no interest." Another says, "They take it for granted that we know everything that is being taught, and so therefore we can't understand what they mean." In these circumstances the students are at best sullen and uncooperative, and they may be tempted into disorder.

No matter how interested a class may be in what they are studying, there comes a time when mental fatigue sets in. Even before that, the need for movement makes some pupils fidget in their seats. Plan the work in blocks, alternating jobs that require high concentration and those that permit talking and moving around.

Skillful classroom management and efficient routine prevent many difficulties with discipline. There ought not to be any considerable amount of time when any pupil does not know what he should be doing. Classes often begin to "fool around" while books and supplies are being passed out or a movie projector is being set up or while the teacher writes questions on the board. One student complains, "He just kept us sitting while he wrote exam questions on the board, and then while he scolded us for being noisy. It cut down our exam time and it really wasn't our fault."

You don't have to operate on a split-second routine, but you do have to give hard thought to how to shift from activity to activity smoothly and easily and how to keep the class occupied meanwhile. You can avoid some delays by doing things yourself ahead of time and others by having students do them while you work with the class. When a delay seems inevitable, take the class into your confidence. Put the problem as you see it up to them, and ask for their suggestions about how it can best be solved.

One pupil shows how lack of understanding creates confusion. He writes: "I think teachers should discuss schoolwork a little more before written work is handed out, so confusion will not start and students won't be asking each other questions." The way out of this difficulty is to think out directions as part of your preparation for a class and even then, after you have given them, to ask the class if there are any questions.

Giving directions is an art in itself, but it's one that can be learned. The first principle is to be sure you have everyone's attention. If, for example, the class is working quietly and a pupil raises a question that applies to the whole class, you can usually secure attention by merely saying, "Charlie has a question." If the class is working rather noisily on a diversity of matters, you need a signal of some sort. Many teachers rap on a desk, and the students soon learn to recognize the sound as a call to order. Gym instructors and coaches use a whistle. (In previous centuries, teachers of one-room schools used a desk bell. We've seen a sweet-toned silver bell inscribed, "To Miss Bartlett with the respectful affection of her pupils,

1828.'' People laugh at bells today, but we regret their passing.) Once you have asked for attention, wait quietly until you have it. The wait may seem long but it's usually quicker and more effective than repeated requests. Word your directions as simply as possible. If you can, put commands positively rather than negatively. The positive command has the merit of giving something to be done, while the negative command may put a new wrong idea into the pupils' heads. The positive approach is exemplified by the request, "Will you please . . . ?" Politeness is always desirable. Use your deepest tone of voice and speak at your normal speed or a little slower. Give the pupils a chance to ask you to explain. If you have the slightest suspicion that anyone has misunderstood you, ask him not only to repeat the directions but to tell you how he is going to carry them out.

Alertness to the mood and the attitude of the class is essential to continued control, even when you are sure that the group as a group and the pupils as individuals like you and wish to cooperate with you. Make a habit of "keeping your tentacles out" so that you can instantly sense any strain. Practically, this means keeping your eyes and ears open. Pause briefly now and then to look and listen with the conscious purpose of assuring yourself that everything is all right. If you do, you'll be quick to note when the class is becoming bored or restless. Do they need a change? What about temperature? light? ventilation? Step out into the corridor a minute and then, when you return to the room, take a sniff. (A principal took his four-year-old daughter with him when he had to go to the high school on an errand. The little girl informed a senior, "This is Daddy's school." "Oh, no," said the senior, "it's Mr. Raymond's school." To which the little girl replied, "It smells just like Daddy's school.") If you find you are neglecting to check physical conditions, and perhaps anyway, appoint students to check them for you.

The alert teacher who habitually keeps his eye on the whole class very soon knows what pupils neglect work and entice others, actively or by example, into disorder. On the other hand, the teacher who pays more attention to paper work and textbooks than to his pupils is courting trouble. A high-school sophomore writes: "I have only one class that is not quiet. Two boys sit together in the rear of the room and talk constantly and never do their classwork. They cause everyone to turn around and look at them and laugh and make remarks, and the teacher thinks it is the whole class that is causing the disturbance when she's not looking, and so she blames everyone. She has not found out that it's only two students, and of course no one is going to tell her. I think she should try to be more observing and find the real troublemakers and put them up in front where she could watch them." And a senior writes: "In math class the teacher cannot catch the kids that are causing the trouble. They throw erasers, pencils, and protractors when his back is turned or when he is helping one of the students."

You can see your class better if you stand up and move around the room rather than sit like a sphinx behind your desk. If you are standing where you can see a pupil, you can usually sense when he is going to do something he shouldn't and forestall the aberration very simply. Almost always he will be watching you, if only out of the corner of his eye. It's easy to let him know that you are aware of his intentions.

A smile at the incipient troublemaker is an effective means of control. It lets him know that you know what he is up to, it does not call the rest of the class's attention to him, and it keeps the atmosphere friendly. In the last respect, it's better than a frown. When you think a pupil is starting to make trouble, you can be practically sure of maintaining control if you will move quietly and stand near him. Another common expedient, useful during a recitation, is to direct a sudden question about the lesson at the inattentive or restless student. He'll probably say he doesn't know the answer. Don't press the matter, because that would call undue attention to him, and attention may be what he wants. Sometimes you'll have to call an offending student sharply by name to bring him back to order. Remember to keep your voice deep. Avoid sarcasm. It's very easy to make a fool of an inattentive pupil, but in the long run it doesn't pay in your relations with him or with the class.

THE CONFERENCE ON MISBEHAVIOR

When ordinary methods of control do not keep a pupil from misbehaving, arrange to talk with him about what he has done and about his attitude. This is a necessary step whether he is a chronic offender or a pupil who is temporarily excited by the possibilities he sees in some bit of mischief or disobedience. As soon as you sense that he is doing something he shouldn't, say quietly but firmly, "Don, please come to see me here after school." This serves notice on both Don and the class that you will not ignore a challenge. Promptness and firmness here, as elsewhere, usually prevent disorder from spreading.

Pupils, especially older pupils, regard the conference as one of the fairest and most effective means of discipline. Again and again they praise the teacher who "showed me why it was wrong" or "made me want to do better" and "was nice in the way he handled it." But a good conference is not easy to manage, particularly when it comes early in the year before you have had time to learn much about the pupil.

Our reports from teachers and pupils and our own talks with difficult pupils suggest some specific cautions and some methods that may help you conduct a conference well. We take up the don't's first.

Don't scold. Don't try to reason while you or the pupil or both of you are angry; wait until you cool down, until the next day if necessary. Don't keep a pupil so long that you interfere with another class, his chance to get out at recess, his lunch, or his employment or another engagement after school. Don't ask the pupil to admit he was wrong or to apologize or to promise not to offend again. Don't threaten—a conference is not a punishment or a prelude to punishment.

If you can, have two chairs ready, instead of sitting behind your desk and having the pupil stand. Come right to the point. The pupil almost surely knows why you want to talk to him, and there is no point in beating around the bush. A good start is to say, "Sit here beside me. You and I have to understand each other better. Your talking to Ed this morning when I was explaining to the class what I wanted done shows you haven't learned how students should treat teachers." Then pause to give him a chance to state his side, especially if another pupil was involved. There is sometimes a possibility that you have misjudged him, and students bitterly resent unfairness. If what he says strikes a corresponding chord in you, you may say, "I know how you feel. I've felt that way myself. But we can't let ourselves act on our feelings."

Probably the pupil will say nothing. In that case, explain very briefly your reasons for disapproving what he did. Let him know that you feel strongly on the subject, if you can do this without scolding. Try to show him how the way he has misbehaved might handicap him out of school, or, better, how the opposite kind of behavior might help him. For example, you can stress the value of good manners in making and keeping friends and in holding a job. Try to close in a friendly but positive manner: "I'm here to help you learn. That's what you come to school for. So I don't expect anything like this to happen again. I'd like to have you talk with me a few minutes before class next Monday. We'll see how you are getting along and how I can help. Is that convenient for you?"

Closing a conference by making a definite appointment for another conference assures the pupil of your continuing interest. He feels not only that you will keep a check on his behavior but also that you are willing to pay attention to him. He almost certainly craves attention and approval. The interlude gives him a chance to earn it, and the appointment the hope of receiving it. Do your best not to disappoint him.

THE SHIFT TO INFORMALITY

Once you are sure of your class's desire to cooperate and of your ability to control the group and the individuals in the group, you will probably begin to be much more informal. Usually this is not a matter of conscious decision on your part, but rather the unconscious result that follows when you and the class have learned to work together. You are all friends, and treat each other like friends.

The amount of informality that develops in your classroom is of course affected by many conditions: the rules of the school, the size of the school, the age of your pupils, the size of the class, the type of activity, the time at your disposal, the abilities of the pupils, and, perhaps most important, the kind of discipline to which you and your class have been accustomed. If you and the class have been used to formal methods, you should shift to informality quite slowly and carefully. The prerequisite is that you yourself be convinced that more informality will best serve the interests of your pupils and the objectives of the curriculum.

We ourselves have no doubt that the pupils of a good informal teacher learn more and develop more self-discipline than do the pupils of a good formal teacher. Young children need the freedom of informality, including the freedom to move about. Older students need the practice in managing themselves.

High-school classes are traditionally more formal than elementary classes. But high-school students who have some formal and some informal teachers are quite articulate about the advantages of informality. Here are some of their opinions: "Well, this business of having to ask permission to speak is all right sometimes. But I think when two pupils are talking quietly, not disturbing anyone, the teacher should allow them to go on talking." "If teachers could allow informality without letting the class get out of hand, classes would be much more enjoyable as well as instructive. In some classes, the teacher has absolutely no control and allows the students to do practically whatever they want, including answering back. In others, an army type of discipline governs. If discipline could be somewhere in between, it would be much better." "Discipline in the classroom depends on the teacher. The teacher who mingles with the class holds your attention." "If there were more time for teachers and students to get to know one another better and to discuss their difficulties, there would be no differences."

"Some teachers really put quite a lot of confidence in you. They make you feel part of the school, which is as it should be."

If you decide to shift to informal procedures, your first step is to discuss the possibility with your class. Be sure that they know why you think a shift desirable, that they sincerely agree and are willing to do their part, and that they understand that if the system—or perhaps we should say lack of system—doesn't work well, you will have to revert to formality until they show that they can manage themselves. For example, if you have been requiring students to raise a hand and be recognized before volunteering an opinion, ask the class how they would feel about trying to conduct a discussion as adults would, that is, with each contributing as he sees the need and opportunity but being very careful to be courteous to everyone else. If they agree, warn them that there may be some hitches at first, but that you'll extend the learning period as long as they are trying. At the end of the first informal discussion, take a few minutes to tell them what you think they did well. Then ask them to say what they think they could have done better. This sort of evaluation is an excellent stimulus to general observation as well as to improvement. And it has the merit of bringing group pressure to bear on the excessive talker. If after a fair trial you feel that informality doesn't work well, return to your previous methods for a week or two. Then try informality again. This time the class may be more cooperative. If your trial is successful, you can discuss with your students other problems of class management and routine, and little by little substitute pupil self-direction for teacher domination.

Giving students freedom to talk and move about the room is in many teachers' minds synonymous with informality. Certainly such freedom under appropriate safeguards is typical of informal classrooms. Your two guides to how much freedom to allow are courtesy and convenience. There is no need for a pupil to raise his hand for permission to take part in a discussion, if he politely refrains from interrupting another student and doesn't talk so much that he keeps others from having a turn. There's no need to ask permission to consult the big dictionary or to fetch paper, if the errand doesn't become the occasion for bumping into others or lingering to satisfy curiosity about others' work. If you have divided your class into groups so that some are working with you while others are working independently, allowing students to decide when they need to talk to each other and to move about is exceedingly convenient. You are relieved of interruption and students are saved delays. Thousands of teachers manage their classrooms in this informal manner, and their students do as much or more work than those who are subject to rigid restrictions.

Not only talking and moving about the room, but the organization and conduct of group work, entering and leaving the room when periods shift, going to the library, going to the toilet—any and all of scores of decisions that must be made in the course of a school day can be wisely made by pupils who are really trying to profit from schoolwork. Of course, you and your students have to consider conditions in the school, for example, whether or not the librarian can accommodate extra workers at a particular time, and the rules of the school, for example, that a record is to be kept of all students who leave the room and why. But the more decisions pupils make for themselves, the more you escape from burdensome detail and the more they learn to be responsible.

SELF-DISCIPLINE

The goal of all discipline is self-discipline.

An experienced secondary-school teacher of French who was starting in a new school writes:

The students in East High School have decided that I'm all right. I had a taste of what a young teacher must face during his first weeks. Luckily there is a vacant room across the hall. When I spotted a disturber I had him take his work over there. This deprived him of the chance to make "oral points," that is, to earn credits for volunteering answers, which in itself I've found an effective means of securing effort, attention, and participation in French conversation. And now, suddenly, there are no discipline problems. The kids are just trying to learn French. I went visiting on Wednesday, and the four teachers who took my classes reported that the class presidents ran each group very well. I've set up committees to help plan the work and class officers to manage routine. It's more time-consuming than when I do it as a dictator—but so far it seems to be very effective. One of the best results is that the students actually accept and do the homework that the committees plan.

You will note that this teacher did not abdicate. He was quick to punish a disturber. But he was willing to enlist a class's help in the management of the room and in seeking the solution to the problem of homework—a problem that is at the root of much disobedience and hard feeling on the part of students. Once more we see that there is no conflict between friendliness and firmness.

Having students share the management of the classroom is a logical development from informality. The students, having learned to be responsible for themselves, now take on the larger responsibility of seeing that the life and work of the group move smoothly, pleasantly, and efficiently.

Many elementary-school teachers start each day with a class planning session. The schedule for the day and the activities of individuals and groups are discussed briefly, and an outline of conclusions is placed on the board. Another brief session at the end of the day (or a few minutes at the beginning of the next morning's planning session) is given over to evaluating how well plans have been carried out. Secondary-school sub-ject-matter teachers may feel that the short period does not leave time for this type of planning by the group. However, many high-school home-room teachers have worked with their classes to build a room organization to carry out recurring duties such as the collection of club dues. And both home-room and subject-matter teachers have found it valuable to enlist the students' cooperation in working out problems, such as how to start and stop work with a minimum waste of time. Many teachers at all levels who have been dissatisfied with the discipline in their rooms have found that it improved when the class compared the disadvantages of disorder with the advantages of good order.

An occasional class session ought to be devoted to the broad aspects of discipline: to the objectives that good order pro-motes, to the need of self-discipline in life, and to "good dis-cipline" as a synonym for "good morale." This sounds very serious, but it may be very cheerful, particularly if the class is proud of past achievements and hopes to do even better in the future. Good morale is an active force. The class or the army that has it is never content to rest on its laurels.

THE STUDENT COUNCIL

Someone has said that no school should copy its system of student government from another. This is because only a sys-tem that is worked out by the student body as a whole will en-list the support of all the students. Moreover, all government rests upon the consent of the governed. Merely to substitute student-council regulations for those of the principal and faculty is worse than useless. And to expect students to take over the enforcement of teacher-made rules is foolish. Even a well-established organization like the AAA Safety Patrol de-pends for success upon thorough discussion of its purpose and general agreement to abide by the regulations.

The well-organized student council, particularly in the large secondary school, can do inestimable service. It is generally made up of a group of student leaders, and though some of these will be more popular than bright, there is a strong probability that most of the members will be able. If they are properly encouraged, they will feel responsible. A principal who has a group like this with whom he can talk out problems of school discipline and morale is extremely fortunate.

Most councils are elected, but this in itself is not a guarantee that they represent student opinion. There must be some system to facilitate the flow of criticism and suggestion from the student body as a whole to the council. And there should be some provision for the student body, as a whole or group by group, to discuss the measures the council recommends. One standard device is home-room representation coupled with home-room periods devoted to discussion of council recommendations. Each home room serves as a sort of lower house. Another device is the referendum on proposals made by the council.

TRUST AND RESPONSIBILITY

You cannot legally or morally delegate your authority and your responsibility to the students in your care. You are, according to the law, in the position of the parent as long as a child is in your charge. But, like the good parent, you can show the boys and girls in your room that you like them and mean to help them. You can trust them, and be quite sure that they will merit your trust. They will early prove that, when their time comes to assume responsibility for themselves, they will not be found wanting. One of the clippings in our files reads: "Louisville, Ky. Snow and ice caused delays in the arrival of 22 teachers at the Sallie B. Rutherford Elementary School but classes went on just the same. Their jobs were taken over by 22 11-year-olds, members of the school's 'Teachers of Tomorrow' program. Opening exercises had been completed and lessons were under way when the teachers arrived, one at a time."

POINTS TO REMEMBER

Be yourself—your best self. Keep in the best possible physical health. Get enough rest and recreation. Look your best. Cultivate good manners and avoid unpleasant mannerisms.

Be good at your job. Good teaching depends on a liking for youngsters of the age you teach, enthusiasm for your subject, knowledge of methods and techniques, and a desire to help each and every pupil.

Make your room attractive.

Keep a watchful eye on physical conditions—light, ventilation, temperature, and seating.

Know your pupils as individuals. Know their strengths and weaknesses, the difficulties they face at home, their interests and ambitions. Adjust the curriculum to individual differences.

Keep your students busy and interested. Be sure that each pupil has goals which are served by his schoolwork and that he understands the connection.

Be fair, firm, and friendly.

Be alert.

Remember that the goal of all discipline is self-discipline.

Books and Pamphlets to Read

Behavior and Misbehavior, A Teacher's Guide to Action, by James L. Hymes, Jr. Prentice-Hall, Inc., Englewood Cliffs, New Jersey, 1955.

Discipline for Today's Children and Youth, by George V. Sheviakov and Fritz Redl. Association for Supervision and Curriculum Development, Washington 6, D. C., 1957.

The Discipline of Well-Adjusted Children, by Grace Langdon and Irving W. Stout. John Day Co., New York, 1952.

Teacher Opinion on Pupil Behavior, 1955-56, Research Bulletin, Vol. XXXIV, No. 2, April, 1956. National Education Association, Washington, 1956.

Teaching--An Exciting Challenge, Bulletin 70. Connecticut State Department of Education, Hartford, 1955.

Topics for Study and Research

The disciplinary difficulties of beginning teachers. Case histories and diaries to help determine why some teachers have difficulties and others do not, and particularly the relation of the content and methods of teachers-college curricula to the success of the beginning teacher.

Group dynamics and classroom morale. Why are some groups cooperative and enthusiastic and others, apparently matched as to ability and background, disorderly?

School and Community Projects

Faculty planning to avoid disorder and to cultivate high morale and self-discipline among the students.

Community planning to make schools in underprivileged districts as good in every way as those in favored districts.

PTA Meeting

Film: Maintaining Classroom Discipline. McGraw-Hill Book Company, Text-Film Department, 330 West 42nd St., New York 36, N.Y.

Topic: Classroom discipline today and yesterday.

III

What about Punishment?

Last year my teacher used to lecture us on undertone, and at my table were eight girls and we set an example of what undertone meant. I would yak-yak-yak all day long. That was my trouble, talking. My teacher would keep me after school. I would feel she was doing the right thing. She would never send me to the office or scold me but would explain to me and the other girls how hard it is when 31 children in a room whisper all at once.

—An elementary-school pupil.

Last year I was talking and the teacher caught me. I myself knew other children had talked much more than I but were excused. The teacher isolated me among the girls. Why didn't she isolate the other children? Grudge? I thought what the teacher did was unfair.

—An elementary-school boy.

I took something I should not have taken. She wouldn't let me help her any more and she said she wouldn't be my friend. I felt awful.

—An elementary-school pupil.

There is one thing that teachers do that can get on the nerves of students and that is to yell first and not ask questions.

—A high-school student.

In one class the teacher always threatens to give detention to those who disturb others but he never does. The pupils in this class see that he is easy and take advantage of him.

—A high-school student.

Students who really want to learn something never can because of the clown in the class. When the teacher asks him politely to keep quiet—he'll only make more noise. To improve this the teacher should be stern—like sending the clown to the office after the first warning, or extra assignments, detention for a week, and even make him wash all the blackboards in the school. This would be good when he writes smut on the blackboards.

—A high-school student.

The kids are sent to the office and lectured for a while and then sent back to the rooms to do it all over again. Better give detention, and if they don't come or don't behave in detention, suspend them and go see their parents and have them talk with their minister or priest.

—A high-school student.

If only the teachers said what they mean and stuck to what they said the kids wouldn't fool as much.

—A high-school student.

When, despite your attempts to show him why he shouldn't and despite your efforts at control, a pupil deliberately misbehaves in your classroom, you almost certainly impose a punishment of some kind. If he continues to misbehave, you may tend to resort to ever-more-severe punishments. If you are consistent in punishing his wrongdoing, you expect that the offender will mend his ways in order to escape the inevitable penalties. You hope that other pupils, seeing the consequences of misbehavior, will refrain from it. At least, you fear that, if you allow one pupil's misdemeanors to go unpunished, his classmates will be all too ready to follow his bad example.

THEORY OF PUNISHMENT

Psychology confirms the common-sense observation that we tend to avoid actions that are associated with pain. Effective punishment is essentially a matter of conditioning. Experiments have shown that conditioning is established most quickly and lasts ·longest when the associated stimuli and reactions are closely connected in time, are always connected, and are always connected with a result that the individual wishes to achieve or avoid. You can remember all of this by considering the proverb, "The burnt child fears the fire." The burn comes quickly, it is inevitable, and it is most assuredly to be avoided. Punishment, therefore, should be prompt, consistent, and real. It can be surer than reasoning, because there is less probability of misunderstanding on the child's part.

There is good reason to believe that the mature person's sense of right and wrong and his habit of doing what seems to him right follow on childhood experiences of suffering for wrongdoing. Robert J. Havighurst and Hilda Taba, in their book Adolescent Character and Personality, have shown that youths with good character have commonly been subjected to consistent discipline at home. Havighurst and Taba conclude that consistent discipline is a potent factor in good character because "the child learns that certain behavior will always be followed by punishment, even though light punishment."

Punishment, however, is not always effective. It is ineffective when the child does not associate it with a specific cause, when it is long postponed, when the pain is nonexistent or slight (for example, when the pupil has a good time in detention hall), or when the pain has been foreseen and deliberately risked in order to accomplish a desired result. Punishment is most ineffective when it serves the same end as the behavior that occasioned it. Moreover, there are certain pun-

ishments which may cause more damage to the child than cur-
ing his misbehavior warrants.

LIMITATIONS AND SAFEGUARDS

Very obviously there are some boys and girls for whom
punishment alone does not work, and some who misbehave
more and more despite repeated punishment. In these cases, a
punishment may actually be a contributing cause to misbehavior because it may aggravate the original difficulty or
satisfy in a perverted way an emotional need of the child or do
both. For example, if you punish a youngster who is misbehaving because he does not receive affection and recognition
at home, he feels more acutely than ever that he is not wanted,
but at the same time he feels for the moment that he is the center of attention.

The purpose of punishment is to prevent the recurrence of
misbehavior. Therefore, when a pupil continues to misbehave
despite having been punished, repeated punishment is futile.
Increasing the severity of the punishment may stop a given
form of misbehavior but may drive the pupil to other and still
worse forms. Punishment is at best a negative means of control. It is not a substitute for teaching a pupil why he should
behave differently. And it is certainly not a substitute for finding and correcting the causes of misbehavior.

Any punishment that is arbitrary or cruel or prolonged may
damage a child emotionally. It may also cause resentment and
a desire for revenge and therefore make him behave worse
than ever. Unfortunately, a few teachers still use some punishments that violate all the rules of mental hygiene. Standing a
child in the corner, making him wear a dunce's cap, sticking
chewing gum on the tip of his nose, having him crouch in the
dark hole under the teacher's desk, making him stand with an
arm held out in front of him for fifteen minutes—these and like
punishments are relics of the dark ages, but we have proof of
their current use. Money fines of a penny to a nickel are still
in vogue in some schools, and boys with big allowances or
those who can steal fifty cents take advantage of the system
and learn the attitude that money is the arbiter of morals. An
occasional teacher gives a child the "silent treatment"—re-
fuses to speak to him, to call on him, or to answer his questions, until he approaches desperation.

Any punishment that subjects a pupil to shame and the ridicule of his classmates is dangerous and ineffective. One college freshman's paper shows how the smarting resentment at
public shaming lingers. She writes: "When I was a freshman
in high school a teacher gave me a good talking to in front of

the whole class. It was a very embarrassing situation. He should have asked me to stop after class. I honestly believe a teacher would do more for a student if he never embarrassed the student. Students who are scolded in front of other students have a grudge against the teacher."

You can minimize the dangers and retain whatever advantages there are in punishment (including that of helping the nonoffenders control their impulses) if you will be careful to observe a few principles. To be effective, a punishment should be a natural consequence of the offense. It should be prompt. It should be simple and short. It should be applied consistently. Once the penalty is paid, you should not only let bygones be bygones but take the first opportunity to demonstrate to the pupil that his slate is clean and that you like him.

SCOLDING, THREATS, AND WARNINGS

Analysis of thousands of reports on what teachers do in response to pupils' misbehavior shows that the teacher's first reaction is often to scold. High-school students report being scolded relatively more than elementary-school students do, and girls more than boys, but students of all ages and both sexes are subjected to scoldings. The students rarely use the word "scolding." They are more likely to say, "He hollered at me," or "yelled at me," or "gave me a good talking to." Teachers generally use the word "reprimand," but also say "scold" and "lost my temper." Both pupils' and teachers' reports frequently couple threats with scoldings.

A scolding does serve emphatic notice on a pupil that you disapprove of his behavior. That is the only thing that can be said in its favor. It early degenerates into a habit. Then it has no effect as a deterrent to misbehavior, but it does make the student dislike the teacher and perhaps laugh at him.

Threats have several disadvantages. A threat may be very inconvenient to carry out, but if it is not fulfilled the offender loses his respect for the teacher's authority. Moreover, the threat is powerful only as it pictures a future punishment, and the fact that there is no immediate penalty generally makes the threat ineffective. But sometimes a pupil worries so much over what is going to happen to him that he forgets what it was he wasn't to do. Therefore, when a pupil has misbehaved deliberately and knowingly, an immediate assignment of a penalty is both more effective and less damaging than a threat.

A "fair warning" is not a threat if the teacher has reason to suspect that misbehavior was due to ignorance, carelessness, or true forgetfulness. When these conditions exist, the pupil needs an explanation of why what he did was wrong and why a penalty may follow the next slip.

DETENTION

"Keeping in" is still the punishment favored by almost all teachers. Detention is a convenient form of punishment, which can be simply varied in amount in proportion to the gravity of offenses and which is generally accepted as proper by pupils and by parents. These qualities obscure some disadvantages and some dangers in customary variations.

Just to sit with folded hands for a few minutes after school is not much more than a token penalty. As such, it serves to let a young child feel he has squared accounts, and it therefore helps him be cheerful and cooperative. But keeping a youngster in for a considerable period of time or day after day or during recess or during the lunch period, all interfere with the rest and release he needs, and may cause further misbehavior. Afternoon detention may be impossible because of bus schedules. It may upset parents who expect a child home at a given time. In the case of high-school students it may interfere with after-school employment. To postpone the detention period to the following day, so that the pupil can notify parents or employers, violates the principle of promptness, though there may be no alternative. (Some schools escape the parent-employment difficulty by having "detention" periods before school in the morning.) If a pupil has nothing to do in detention period, and particularly if several are kept in together, their idle hands —and tongues—are ready for mischief. Students from one high school which has a "detention room"(so that a teacher can assign detention without having to stay after school himself) report that the behavior in that room is "twice as bad as in class."

Some teachers get around the idleness problem by requiring extra work. The students copy sentences or write essays or do math problems during detention period. This is bad because it associates study with punishment. (Note that students who copy a sentence 500 or more times, presumably correctly, may misspell a word in the sentence when they report it, e.g., "He made me write, 'I will not deserve dentition again,' 1000 times.")

The best use of detention is to keep a student in to make up time he has willfully wasted, to complete classwork he has deliberately left unfinished, or to do neglected homework. Under these circumstances it is a natural consequence of his failure. He may learn a lesson that will be valuable when he works for a living. If you keep a student in to finish work, try tutoring him a bit in it. This shows your willingness to help, and he may change his attitude.

SENDING TO THE PRINCIPAL

Boys of all ages report being sent to the principal almost as frequently as they do being kept after school. Secondary-school girls report it only occasionally, and elementary-school girls very rarely. Apparently the unruly boy is difficult for many classroom teachers to control, and his behavior may be so aggressive that it upsets the whole class. The only sure relief is to get him out of the room, and the principal's office is generally the only place where he can be kept under observation. (Some schools have "quiet rooms," usually under supervision of a teacher, to which students are sent. The time of return may be left to the student, who is told to come back when he feels he can behave.) To send a chronic offender to the hall or cloakroom, where he can scrawl obscenities on the walls, play practical jokes with other students' belongings, and entice passersby into trouble, is to invite disaster. Even when a boy is sent to the office, it is wise to have some system that makes sure he reports there without delay and returns straight to the classroom when he is supposed to. Otherwise he may hide out in a toilet room or even leave school.

Many teachers consider sending a pupil to the principal a sign of weakness. Some principals discourage the practice because they dislike the feeling that they must support the teacher, right or wrong—which pupils accuse them of doing—or, still worse, must referee between pupil and teacher. But surely one of the principal's responsibilities is to help control and rehabilitate chronic offenders. If you have one in your class, you should consult with the principal and be sure what he wishes you to do when a student defies your ordinary measures of control.

The principals and supervisors of the Philadelphia public schools have worked out a set of guides to govern the principals' contacts with unruly students and their parents. The five major steps in the interview with the student are given as: (1) Make sure that the student knows exactly why he has been referred; (2) Afford the student a chance to tell his side of the story; (3) Let the student know the principal's judgment concerning the matter at issue; (4) Make the student aware that a record is kept of the case; (5) Require the student to review the corrective measures worked out in his case. In addition, a cardinal principle "requires that the principal dismiss the student with a clearer understanding of his problems, an added incentive to bring about their solution, and a conviction of the principal's constructive intent." The principal must keep the teacher informed and work closely with him in developing and carrying out plans. The principal should show his interest in the progress of the student by greeting him cordially when they meet, finding opportunity for the student to work for him, dropping into his class, conferring with him, and encouraging him in his progress. The teacher should refrain from public criticism of the student, particularly in the presence of the principal. (See Discipline for Constructive Citizenship, Administrative Bulletin No. 22B, School District of Philadelphia, 1955.)

CHANGING A STUDENT'S SEAT

You may think of changing a student's seat more as a corrective action than as a punishment. The student generally considers it a punishment. But, though he may feel ashamed at his classmates' knowing that he has had to move, he generally recognizes the fairness and even the wisdom of the treatment. A fourth-grader remarks, "I couldn't help talking to Alice, so he helped me by shifting us." You need to keep some precautions in mind. Putting a youngster in a seat apart from everybody makes him a cynosure. He's tempted to show off, and at the same time he feels shamed and resentful. The idea that the back of the room is the place for offenders derives from the 18th-century "bottom of the class" system. There is some advantage in placing the class clown where others cannot see him. But he can still make himself heard, and you may find it difficult to keep him under observation. So, generally you do better to place him near you. To seat a boy among the girls and vice versa shames the pupil and may make him behave worse. Some teachers report success following a talk with a student in which he is asked if changing his seat might help him change his behavior and then is allowed to decide where to sit. This makes him in a way responsible for improving and gives the teacher a privilege to take away if he continues to be disorderly.

DEPRIVATION

Taking away a privilege that a student has abused or a possession that tempts him into trouble is usually the punishment to fit the crime, and thus fair and effective. A reasonable extension of the idea is that certain privileges are dependent on continued good behavior and good work and may be taken away from a student who doesn't live up to the conditions. A sixth-grader writes: "I ignored my lessons too much. My teacher took me off the school safety patrol. I didn't like it, so I worked harder and got back on." Deprivation, fairly administered, seems to be the most effective of all penalties. The danger in using it in the case of a chronic offender is that the privilege denied him may be one that has been helping him learn responsibility or earn approval. How one teacher saw the dilemma and resolved it is shown in the following report:

Franklin, age 11, a colored boy in Grade V, had improved greatly after I'd suggested to the class that he be made a squad leader. But, because he had broken playground regulations one morning before school, one child in class meeting suggests that Franklin be removed from the position of squad leader. Franklin glances furtively at the speaker. Then he bends his head on his chest and fumbles with his hands. Then he feigns boredom, and looks out the window. Then he glares defiantly. At first I take no part. When the chairman asks Franklin if the accusation is correct he says yes. Then I remind the group that Franklin has been a good leader (his face brightens) and takes good care of playground equipment. He sits up straight for the first time. I continue that I don't like what he did this morning but that perhaps the class should give him another chance. They so vote, and Franklin looks happy and takes part in the rest of the meeting. Following the meeting I spoke firmly to him about his behavior. For the remainder of the day he was happy and relieved and behaved like an angel.

RECTIFICATION AND REPARATION

Making a student do rightly what he has done wrongly (for example, making him go back and walk down the stairs he has taken with a running jump, to the peril of his own and others' limbs) is a natural teaching procedure. It's like having him correct a mistake in an arithmetic example. Similarly, it seems natural to require a student to repair damage he has done accidentally or on purpose. Students regard both procedures as consequences of their behavior and therefore fair. But our materials show a surprising number of incidents in which rectification or reparation would seem to be the only action necessary (for example, when a pupil in painting class accidentally spilled his water cup) which were actually punished by detention or otherwise. Presumably the students involved had irritated the teachers to the point where a separate penalty was thought due.

Even when you don't impose a penalty on a chronic offender in addition to making him rectify a mistake, you may be impatient and scold. But we have a few reports which show that the turning point in previously desperate cases came when the teacher pitched in and helped a pupil clean up or make a repair. You have to be very broad-minded to go to the assistance of a pupil who has deliberately spilled ink. But try it sometime.

SUSPENSION AND EXPULSION

Suspension and expulsion are generally reserved to the principal or superintendent and thus are out of the classroom teacher's province. You may recommend one or the other, but you cannot enforce it. (This means, incidentally, that you should never threaten a pupil with either.) Suspension is sometimes effective in forcing a student or his parents to cooperate, but it must be carefully administered and supervised. There have been surprising lapses where the parents have received no notice and the suspended student has roamed the streets until he got into serious trouble with the police. And there is always the problem of the work that a suspended student misses. Expulsion may be a great benefit to a student when it results in his getting a full-time job or forces his parents to place him in a special school or institution. But in all cases the school has an obligation to follow up the student until placement has been made.

CORPORAL PUNISHMENT

Some individuals and organizations are now advocating a greater use of corporal punishment in schools. Recently a city teachers' association, a state secondary-school principals' association, and a state bar association all independently suggested that schools return to giving "old-fashioned" whippings. Anyone who reads some of the descriptions we have of continued defiance of teachers and principals can sympathize with a desire to try corporal punishment. But research indicates that where corporal punishment is regularly used (as in certain English schools and some American private schools) it is accepted as routine and is no more a deterrent than any other punishment. Students may feel left out if they are not sometimes whipped, and may even boast of the severity of a whipping and the skill of the master who gave it. Nor does corporal punishment seem to have a good effect when it is administered rarely, or as a last resort, or brutally. A junior-high-school principal who formerly used it writes:

> I have not administered corporal punishment in the last fifteen years and have my doubts as to whether it helped reform anyone when we did resort to it. I think in many cases it made for hard feelings. I met a man on the bus whom I had paddled when he attended school here, and he wouldn't speak to me. Some of the boys whom I paddled not only continued to misbehave while here but ended up in reform schools and the state penitentiary. One of them became the "Silk Stocking Bandit" of local fame, and another killed the cashier of a local department store.

The teacher who slaps or whips pupils should be aware of the number of times parents seek redress by court action. The courts usually uphold the teacher, but the experience is bound to be unpleasant. This seems to us a hazard that no teacher is required to run and one whose doubtful benefits do not justify its use. If a school wishes to use corporal punishment, the whipping or paddling should be administered by the principal in front of an adult witness other than the complaining teacher. A written report should be sent to' the superintendent immediately, so that, when the inevitable happens and a board-of-education member telephones him about the parents' (exaggerated) account, the superintendent will have some chance to calm everyone down.

In the rare case in which a student strikes you, you will be tempted to hit back. And there are times when you may feel compelled to use physical force to remove a recalcitrant pupil from the room or to restrain his movement. Except in a clear case of protecting another pupil, you do far better to summon help—the principal or the custodian. The Armed Forces, after decades of experience with the discipline of some extremely tough individuals, have a fixed rule that no officer should lay hands on an enlisted man. It's a good rule to remember.

POINTS TO REMEMBER

An ounce of prevention is worth tons of punishment. Be sure that you are using methods that will minimize the occasions for disorder. The alert teacher can usually control disorder before it reaches the stage where punishment is necessary.

Be fair, firm, and friendly.

Don't punish a whole class for the misbehavior of individuals in it. Very seldom, if ever, is every pupil involved. When two or three pupils are fighting or talking or shoving each other, it's often the course of wisdom to punish all three equally. If you try to referee, you'll never learn the whole story.

Never scold, threaten, ridicule.

Be consistent.

Be prompt.

Keep the penalty to the minimum that you judge will be effective. Avoid all unusual, long, and cruel punishments.

Let the punishment fit the crime. Deprivation of a possession or privilege that has been abused and rectification or reparation are the two kinds of action that most frequently fulfill this condition.

Be sure that the pupil understands why he is being punished. Give him a chance to state his case.

Let bygones be bygones.

Always hunt for the causes of misbehavior. If disorder is general, the cause may be in bad conditions or a poor curriculum. It may be in your attitude or methods. But the most frequent problem is that of the chronic offender who is driven by circumstances beyond his control. His reform depends not on punishment but on constructive action.

Books and Pamphlets to Read

Adolescent Character and Personality, by Robert J. Havighurst and Hilda Taba. John Wiley & Sons, Inc., New York, 1949.

Child Training and Personality, by J. W. M. Whiting and I. R. Child. Yale University Press, New Haven, 1953.

Discipline for Constructive Citizenship, Administrative Bulletin Nos. 22, 22A (Supplement A, For Classroom Teachers), and 22B (Supplement B, For School Principals). School District of Philadelphia, 1955.

Topics for Study and Research

The immediate and long-range effects of various forms of punishment. How and how often were chronic offenders punished in prior years? A comparison of the present behavior of pupils who have been treated permissively at home or at school with those who have been consistently punished for deliberate misbehavior.

School and Community Projects

A study, under the auspices of the Juvenile Court, of the punishments that have been inflicted at home and in school on children who later became delinquent.

PTA Meeting

Films: First Lessons; Angry Boy. Mental Health Film Board, 166 East 38th St., New York 16, N. Y.

Topic: Spanking.

IV

The Teacher and the Individual

George, age 8, Grade III, IQ 104, is our class wanderer, pugilist, and trumpet. His parents are getting a divorce. The other children dislike him. How can I help him become better liked? Using him as an errand boy or helper results in his becoming wild and aggressive. Ignoring his loud remarks results in his talking still louder and more frequently. Having George sit next to me keeps him happy but doesn't help him become a member of the group. He still makes comments, but at least he does not disturb the other children.
—A teacher.

Harry, age 16, a high-school sophomore, IQ 125, has improved much this year. He is still constantly in "hot water," but his goals are more realistic. Unfortunately his parents don't grasp the seriousness of the situation, and there are still frustrating circumstances at school. I am, however, hopeful, perhaps because I do want to see him turn out well. I started the year thinking he was a nuisance, and wishing the principal had not sent him to me. Now, after six months' overtime work, I actually like the boy.
—A teacher.

Ike started last year as a junior. He was 17, and though he had an IQ of 92 he had no interest in schoolwork. He did enjoy making all kinds of trouble. Nothing his teachers and the principal could do had any effect. We urged him to leave school, and even got him the promise of a job. He said he preferred not to work! We asked the administration to expel him, but the family objected. So in May we promoted him to the senior class and graduated him in June. If this was a sin, the end justified the means. How heavenly school seems this year!
—A teacher.

When simple control, reasoning, and ordinary penalties fail to keep a pupil from misbehaving, you know you are face to face with a problem of some dimensions. The sooner you start to plan possible solutions, the better, because continued misbehavior on the pupil's part and increasingly severe punitive actions on yours may strain relations to the point where there is little you can do. And you must remember that other teachers have probably tried to coerce the chronic offender into good behavior and obviously failed. You must also remember that there is little chance of any quick change in the pupil's fundamental attitudes. Perhaps the most difficult task any teacher

37

can face is that of controlling the behavior of a chronic offender while trying to find the causes of his misbehavior, to work out remedies, and to help him learn to overcome his difficulties.

MAINTAINING OBJECTIVITY

You are only human if you actively dislike a pupil who continually disrupts your class. Antagonism stirs antagonism and violence, violence in any human relation. This very fact explains why many youngsters who get off on the wrong foot with their teachers never regain step. The teacher takes the misbehavior personally, and mutual hostility increases rapidly.

The defense against this attitude in yourself and therefore in a pupil is the realization that his bad behavior is not, in the beginning at least, actually directed at you. The individual pupil who seems to hate you, who says and thinks he does hate you, and who treats you with angry impertinence or sullen resistance in class and writes obscene remarks about you on the corridor walls does not as a rule hold a personal grudge against you. The exception comes when he believes that you have been unfair. But at the start, anyway, he hates you only as a symbol. If he has been frustrated by his inability to do schoolwork, you are the obvious target of the aggression his frustration generates. Or he may hate you as a symbol of authority, as he hates all teachers, policemen, clergymen, and parents. And he probably began by hating his parents. Sometimes, though his actions belie it, he may like you better than anyone else, and underneath may be looking to you to keep him from behaving the way he does. He doesn't know that his apparently willful actions are due to emotional maladjustment or to a physical condition or to a combination of the many possible causes. He only knows that he feels compelled to act as he does and that he hopes you can prevent him.

As you learn more about a pupil and gain a more definite understanding of why he behaves as he does, you will find it easier to treat his disorder matter-of-factly. In the meantime you can do much to avoid antagonism toward the pupil if you talk with other teachers who have had him or have other pupils who behave in the same ways. Their experiences may convince you that the misbehavior is not a manifestation of personal dislike of you. And knowing that others have the same kind of problem is reassuring to you.

Some good teachers say that they do not wish any information, either scholastic or behavioral, about a pupil whom they are to have in class. They say that the pupil ought to be able to start with a clean slate. Therefore they never consult the previous teachers of their classes or study the cumulative records. The only valid argument in favor of this position is that it reflects a determination to be fair and open-minded. There are many arguments on the other side. Ignorance may lead you to perpetuate the cause of the trouble, notably to expect of a pupil scholastic work that he is unable to do. Moreover, you can no more escape knowing when you have a pupil who has caused other teachers in your school difficulty than you can avoid breathing the heavy, sultry air that precedes a hurricane. If you haven't already heard about the pupil's escapades, a colleague is sure to greet you with, "I hear you've got the holy terror this year."

You certainly want to know about a hard-of-hearing or myopic child before you begin to teach him. Without such knowledge, you may attribute his errors to stupidity or laziness or dislike of you as a teacher. You may not discover the true cause of his difficulties until he has fallen hopelessly behind. But if you know about his handicaps ahead of time, you do everything you can to help him start well and keep up. The chronic offender is in much the same case. If you know about him, you begin by working with him and so avoid mutual antagonism.

ESTABLISHING RAPPORT

Good rapport with a disorderly pupil increases the probability that you will be able to help him. And even if all your efforts lead only to failure, good rapport makes the interval less unpleasant for everyone concerned. A certain inmate of a federal penitentiary who is serving a long term for armed robbery of a post office is still remembered with a sort of amused affection by his former teachers and by the school officials who struggled to prevent his downfall. The boy was good-looking and a good athlete. He had an IQ somewhat below normal, and he was handicapped by the early desertion of his father, the death of his mother, and years of association with a bad gang. He lived with his grandmother in a slum district. She spoke little English and had no control over him. He was already on probation when he transferred to public school as a seventh-grader in junior high school. In his first week in school he had a fist fight in a classroom, stole money from a pupil's locker, and deliberately threw a ball through a window. Each of these offenses was punished. If they had been reported to the court, the boy's probation would probably have been canceled. But the principal and the teachers decided that they would see if they couldn't save the boy. They worked out a plan of trying to capitalize on his athletic interests (the gym teacher made himself responsible for the boy and scheduled him for extra periods) and of making friends with him. They took every chance they could to talk with him and work with him when he was behaving well. To their surprise, they found that he was really a likable youngster. He responded by liking them and behaving better for them. But the gang was too much. He was caught by the police in a robbery and sent to a school for delinquents. His teachers and principal were sorry to see him go: sorry for their failure and sorry to lose the boy.

The key to establishing good rapport is association with the pupil when he is not in trouble. Coaching him in some extracurricular activity or even in one of his weak subjects is a good means of bringing him closer to you. One of the best is to accept him as a volunteer helper for a chore that you do after school. A boy who is helping you decorate a Christmas tree can become very confidential.

But you should not leave contacts to chance opportunities. Try to arrange brief, informal conferences once or twice a week. The first may grow out of a conference on misbehavior, but if you know you are dealing with a chronic offender, a meeting with him before he begins to cause trouble lets you start as friends. Time and place will depend on what grade you teach and whether or not you use methods that include routine conferences with all of your pupils in class time or in "free" periods. You don't want the conferences to be a burden to him or to take him away from games with his friends. But, even if you are not fortunate enough to have a schedule that provides periods for conferences, a survey of your duties and his normal routine will probably reveal a few minutes in the week when you can regularly get together. A short meeting before school in the morning or at noon can work wonders.

At first, at least, your principal problem may be to induce the pupil to talk freely. Prior information is obviously useful here. If you know from the study of the records or from papers he has written what his interests, his hobbies, and his hard subjects are, you can ask stimulating questions. General questions may serve: "What do you like to do out of school?" "Have you any brothers and sisters?" "What do you expect to do when you finish school?" If you are aware of the favorite TV programs and are up on the current events in the lives of the pupils in your class, you can almost always discover a spark of interest and nurse it into a flame. "Did you see the parade yesterday? Where were you?"

As the pupil loosens his tongue and begins to talk with you naturally, cultivate the art of listening. The main virtue in the kind of conference we have in mind lies not in the advice you give, nor yet in the information about himself and his problems that the pupil confides. The big benefits are the feeling of release he gets from being able to talk about himself and the assurance he gains from having you, a teacher! treat him as an interesting friend.

MANAGING THE CHRONIC OFFENDER

Your conferences with a disorderly pupil and your efforts to make friends with him may sharply reduce the amount of his misbehavior. At least, if you have progressed to the point where he sincerely wants to do better, he'll respond quickly when you check him. But there is more than a probability that he'll continue to misbehave, despite your best efforts, until you discover and remedy the causes of his behavior. In the meantime you must manage matters so as to prevent as many of his outbreaks as you can and so as to keep him from disrupting the class.

Your actions should be based on the theory that the pupil is under some kind of strain, even though you have no exact knowledge of what the strain may be. Like all of us, he can withstand strain just so long. He may, after he has given way and released the tension, regain control of himself and keep himself in order for minutes, hours, or days. If you observe him carefully, you'll soon learn the symptoms of a pending break. You will also learn how long the intervals between breaks are likely to be. You can then try to relieve the strain at appropriate intervals and thus prevent breaks.

The simple device of asking a question about the lesson may divert the pupil. Other time-tested devices, useful with both older and younger pupils and especially with those who are inclined to overactive, aggressive behavior, include having the pupil pass supplies, sending him on errands, and suggesting that he get a drink of water. One high-school sophomore praises a teacher who "sometimes sends me out to walk around. It makes me feel a lot better." If you know approximately how long a pupil can work quietly, you can talk it over with him and make him responsible for leaving the room periodically.

Seating younger children near your desk often gives them all the support they need. This is more than a matter of their knowing that you will see whatever they do. They seem to draw strength from physical nearness to you. They are rather like a person crossing a narrow bridge. If there is no handrail, he loses balance and falls. But a light rail, even a slender rope that would not hold his weight, gives him the reassurance he needs. If you find that a child does stay out of trouble when he is near you, try alternating periods of keeping him there with periods when you give him work in another part of the room. Experiment with lengthening these. Children do have a way of mastering their own troubles and of learning self-control.

Some disturbed pupils can manage themselves fairly well if they attend school for only part of each day. Arranging part-time attendance requires approval of administrators and the pupil's parents, and perhaps a certificate from a doctor. But even if it does not result in keeping the pupil out of trouble when he is in school, you and your class are relieved of trouble when he is out of school. The relief justifies the effort the arrangements take.

If a part-time schedule cannot be arranged for the compulsively overactive pupil, some system must be devised for getting him out of the classroom for considerable periods of time. The principal's office in a big school sometimes looks like the anteroom of a municipal court on Monday morning, and the principal's clerk often plays the role of deputy sheriff. Keeping a pupil in the office may be the only means a school affords of keeping him out of the regular classroom, and thus be a necessity. Other devices are a "quiet room" under the supervision of a specially chosen teacher, assigning the pupil to extra periods of physical education, and finding active employment for the pupil in the building or on the grounds. The last is very efficacious in the case of older students who can be paid for their labor. Many high schools found that during the depression, when the federal government set up work projects for students in their schools, some of the worst discipline problems evaporated.

SUPPLYING NEEDS

While you are trying to find definite causes of a pupil's difficulties, you should proceed to do everything you can to satisfy all his needs. We call this the "shotgun attack" because the number of pellets in a shotgun's charge gives the marksman a better chance of hitting the target than does the single bullet in a rifle cartridge. But, if you prefer, you can think of it as a multiple-vitamin-with-basic-minerals pill, which is designed to remedy the common deficiencies.

Needs are ordinarily classified as physical and emotional. Physically, a child needs food, rest, clothing, shelter, and movement. The absolute lack of any of these is fatal. A serious deficiency lowers vitality and adversely affects mental activity and emotional stability. Many lists of emotional needs have been compiled. One of the simplest is that of W. I. Thomas: love, security, recognition, and new experiences. Each of these can be enlarged. The child needs to love as well as to be loved. He needs to feel secure in his place in his family's affection, in his standing with his friends, and in his expectation that he will be cared for safely as far ahead as he can see. He needs to be recognized as an individual and to be somebody in his own right; and he needs to feel that his friends recognize his contributions to the group. New experiences, personal and vicarious, physical and intellectual, are essential to a child's growth. Only the child who feels secure will have the courage to adventure, and only the child whose successful ventures are given recognition will continue to seek new experiences.

The parents are the child's primary source of satisfaction for all his needs. If they do not or cannot provide for his physical needs and supply his emotional needs, he must look to adults outside the family. If no one supplements faulty parental care, he will almost surely become a behavior problem and may become seriously maladjusted. The rest of this book is designed to show the principal lacks that cause pupils to be disorderly and to show how the school can counter these difficulties. But while you are working to ascertain what a child's difficulty is, you should assume that everything is wrong and try the shotgun attack. Often you can do such a good job of satisfying a boy's or a girl's needs that you bring about better behavior without ever finding out the true cause of the misbehavior. You may, at the same time, be giving the youngster the emotional strength he must have to win a fight against odds.

The importance of affection is testified to by the old saying, "The good teacher likes children." And the truth of another old saying, "Praise is the magic wand of discipline," rests upon the fact that praise satisfies the need for recognition. One teacher writes: "I've tried everything to change Jack's behavior—talking to him, changing his seat, sending him to the principal—all in vain. So far the only thing that helps is to give him small jobs to do for me and praise him when he does them well."

When teachers try hard to convince a pupil that they like him and really will help him, the effects may be excellent. One teacher writes:

Belle, age 14, Grade IX, IQ 102, has been a problem since the start of seventh grade. She was bold, impertinent, refused to do her work, cut classes, and began to run with a bad crowd. Her parents were called in and said she was just as bad at home and they'd like to send her to reform school. They refused to cooperate with us or with the Family Welfare Society. This year the head counselor, the school dietitian, and I put our heads together to see how we could help. We got Belle a paid job in the school cafeteria. We made it a point to be friendly. She improved a lot. Then at midyears she was shifted to another division and began to misbehave again and gave up the job. The three of us immediately appealed to her and convinced her we were really interested. Now she's back on her job and has been nominated by the school paper for the prize given each year to the pupil who has shown the greatest progress in school spirit and is a credit to the school and the teachers.

THE ATTITUDE OF THE CLASS

Some teachers hesitate to do the kind of thing Belle's teachers did for her because it seems to them to be rewarding bad behavior and they fear that the other pupils in the class will feel resentful. The solution is to enlist the class in your efforts.

The great majority of the classmates of a chronic offender dislike him and dislike his behavior. He is almost sure to get into fights with them, shove and trip them, and knock their books on the floor. They're likely to react in kind and blame him for getting them in trouble. And, because most students do want to learn, they dislike the way the unruly individual interferes with the routine of the class. If the class has had a part in making the rules of the room, they look on his violations as a betrayal.

These feelings more often than not make the misbehaving pupil misbehave worse. When desire for membership in the group and recognition from the group is frustrated, he misbehaves to compel their attention. If he can't be famous he will be notorious. It's a vicious circle.

If you take the class into your confidence and discuss the problem with them when the offender is absent—or in the office—they will almost surely be willing to help you help him. Older students understand the vicious circle very quickly, and even pupils in the second and third grades may show remarkable insight. A first-grade teacher describes how his pupils decided that they'd have to treat a feeble-minded classmate "like he was a baby brother." A third grade discussed the behavior of an attention-seeking girl and concluded that she was spoiled at home; they began to ignore her bossiness but to remind her sharply when she broke a rule, and she quickly learned to conform. When a fourth-grade teacher took the occasion of a difficult pupil's absence to talk over his behavior with the class, one of the pupils remarked: "Perhaps we leave him out of everything on the playground. Perhaps he'd be nicer if we sometimes elected him an officer." They did, and the boy became much easier to live with. A high-school teacher says: "When Ken says something sassy, there's a sudden silence in the room. The other students just look at him, and then go ahead as though nothing had happened. I don't know when they decided on this line, but it's working, and I'm pretending that I don't hear Ken.''

Reaching an agreement with the class on why you are ignoring bad behavior and apparently giving special privileges to some unruly pupils not only prevents misunderstanding of your actions but also gives the class worth-while experience in getting along with others. Thinking out why people behave as they do increases tolerance. And it is excellent motivation to self-control.

ESTABLISHING WORTHY GOALS

If you will compare your best pupils with your poorest, you will almost surely find that the best have definite personal goals in line with the curriculum. This fact differentiates both the orderly from the disorderly and the hard workers from the drifters. A personal goal gives direction to an individual's behavior. A goal serves to integrate his personality, because he gathers together his thoughts and concentrates them on his objective. When a pupil has no conscious objective, or when he thinks the school does not serve his objective or actually interferes with it, he will idle away his school hours drifting from one form of misbehavior to another.

Psychology knows too little about why one youngster picks one goal and another, another. There is a tendency to want to do the things an admired adult does, and therefore it is important for teachers and parents to set a good example. The desire for recognition makes a person want to do something he thinks he can do well, and makes him want to do it better and better. This explains the good effects of the teacher's praising any progress that is related to a goal the teacher would like the pupil to adopt. Rewards in the way of prizes, high marks, honor rolls, and rank are traditional goals in education. They can be powerful motivators of the effort to learn (and to behave) if the pupil believes he can achieve them.

If you know a disorderly pupil's interests and abilities, you have the best chance of helping him establish desirable goals and thus of influencing his behavior for the better. Knowing his interests lets you stir his ambition to achieve immediate and remote goals in line with them and show him how his schoolwork will help him along. Knowing his abilities lets you be sure that his goals are realistic and that there are intermediate objectives he can achieve fairly quickly and thus earn praise for progress. A pupil may be working toward several goals at once

—better marks in arithmetic, a part in the class play, enough money to buy a boat to have at the shore, and a job as an accountant when he grows up. In fact, the happy people of all ages are usually busy trying to fulfill a number of desires, some of which they will satisfy soon and some only after a long time and great effort. The happiest, perhaps, are also striving to forward a great purpose that they cannot expect to see fulfilled in their lifetime.

GATHERING INFORMATION

Whether you are trying general measures like establishing rapport or conducting a detailed search for the causes of misbehavior, you profit from knowing all you can about a pupil's background and about him as a person. You will want to secure all the information you can from the records, from the pupil's previous teachers, from the school nurse, from the pupil himself, and, where possible, from his parents. If you can set this down in a systematic way, it will facilitate your study of the child and it will be an immeasurable help when you confer about the case with your principal, another school official, or an outside specialist. You may feel you have neither the time nor the training to compile the brief case history that we outline below. But the outline is a convenient guide to what to look for and can be useful when you are planning how to help the pupil satisfy his needs.

OUTLINE FOR A BRIEF CASE HISTORY

Teacher's name_____ School_____ Date___
   I. Identifying information. Pupil's name, address, sex, date of birth (verified), age, grade. Father's name, nationality, occupation.
  II. Description of pupil's behavior. A BRIEF statement of what the pupil does that makes this study necessary. (An anecdotal diary of the major incidents on one or two days is excellent.) Secure from the pupil an account of what he has done and how he feels about it.
 III. School history. Age and grade on beginning school. Number of schools attended. Number of years in each grade. Has he skipped any grades? Unusually long absences and reasons for them. Previous teachers' estimates of ability and achievement and their accounts of the pupil's behavior, what they did about it, and results.
  IV. Physical condition. Date and results of last physical examination. Have you knowledge from the records or otherwise of any severe illnesses, accidents, or handi-

caps? Are height and weight about average for age? Are clothing and cleanliness satisfactory? Does he walk, run, jump normally? State what you know about his developmental history, including ages of walking, talking, sex maturation.

V. Mental ability and achievement. Your estimate. Results of standardized group tests: name of test, date given, results. Any special abilities or disabilities? Individual psychological examination? Give date, name and title of examiner, names of tests, results, recommendations.

VI. Interests and occupations. Give favorite subjects and hobbies, part-time or summer employment, educational and vocational ambitions and plans.

VII. Emotional and social status. Relationships with peers. Results of sociograms. Any marked characteristics? Attitudes toward teachers and other adults. Psychiatric examination? Give date, name of physician, recommendations.

VIII. Family relationships and neighborhood conditions. Any information about the emotional tone of the home? If it is a broken or foster home, give details. Describe parent-child relationships and sibling relationships. Describe the home. Has pupil a room of his own? Play space? Describe neighborhood: type, recreation facilities, gangs.

IX. Contact with social agencies and courts. History of the contacts: reasons, results, recommendations.

X. Recommendations. Describe what you think should be done to help the pupil: (a) by you and the school; (b) by his family; (c) by himself.

POINTS TO REMEMBER

While you are trying to keep a chronic offender in order and see that he learns something, or at least doesn't interfere too much with his classmates' learning, you should constantly review your actions and turn over in your mind possible new approaches. You may lie awake thinking and planning, but this is better than having nightmares. Here are some questions to ask yourself:

Am I letting bygones be bygones?

Am I starting each day by being personally friendly, e.g., calling him cheerfully by name when he comes into the room?

Did I give him a chance to talk to me today?

Am I sure he understands what I want him to do?

What are his good points? Am I capitalizing on them?

Am I making any progress in discovering his interests and correlating them with his schoolwork?

Am I alert to the signs of trouble? Is there any way I can forestall it, e.g., by sending him on an errand when he shows signs of restlessness but before he has done something he shouldn't?

Would a change of seat help him to keep out of trouble? Give him a chance to make a new friend?

What were the effects of what I tried today?

Books and Pamphlets to Read

An Application to Education of the Needs Theory, by Louis E. Raths. Modern Education Service, Bronxville, N.Y., 1949.

Becoming, by Gordon W. Allport. Yale University Press, New Haven, 1955.

Classroom Teachers Can Help Maladjusted Children, by N. E. Cutts and Nicholas Moseley. International Council for Exceptional Children, 1201 16th St., N.W., Washington 6, D.C., 1949.

Personality Adjustment of Individual Children, by Ralph H. Ojeman. Department of Classroom Teachers, National Education Association, Washington 6, D. C., 1954.

Topics for Study and Research

Diaries of pupils' behavior and teachers' actions, to determine patterns of behavior and efficacy of actions.

Longitudinal studies of school and later careers of disorderly pupils, e.g., what has happened to a disorderly pupil whom you remember from several years back?

Close study of pupils whose behavior has changed for better or worse during the year, to determine causes, including the effect of teaching procedures.

Descriptions of specific means of motivating better behavior.

School and Community Projects

A committee to make plans for the rehabilitation of disorderly pupils.

Additional clerical help to facilitate the keeping of adequate cumulative records.

Adequate community social services.

PTA Meeting

Film: Mike Makes His Mark. National Education Association, 1201 16th St., N.W., Washington 6, D.C., or your state Education Association.

Topic: The parents' role in school discipline.

V

Illness and Physical Handicaps
as Causes of Misbehavior

Larry, age 10, Grade IV, is the smallest boy in the room. One eye is so badly crossed that he gives the impression of vacancy. Always dirty, he looks forlorn. He always has a chip on his shoulder, and picks fights by pinching and kicking other children. He has the sole school privilege of coming late and leaving early—arranged by the principal after many parents of other children complained of his fighting. On the first day of school his mother told me in front of him how much she disliked him. She and his father both work. They have failed to keep appointments at the clinic to have Larry's eyesight tested. They refuse to have him sent to the sight-saving class in a neighboring city, though our town would pay the fee. Larry never seems to hold a grudge against me, because he knows I like him and would do anything to help him.

—A teacher.

Mac, age 16, a high-school sophomore, has a vile temper, and when he's asked to do something he doesn't particularly like, he becomes angry and stubborn. Unfortunately, our school has little in the way of permanent records. The limited health cards have a list of common childhood diseases (supposedly checked when the child enters kindergarten), weights year by year, and the results of eyesight tests given by the nurse. I didn't know Mac had had epilepsy until a friend of the family told me, thinking it might help me.

—A teacher.

"You poor fish—why didn't they throw you back?"
—A high-school student, taking a shower,
to a boy paralyzed by polio.

Though about one-quarter of our reports from teachers on disorderly children mention some illness or physical defect as a cause of the pupil's difficulties, there are probably many more such cases than teachers realize. Some of the most serious conditions escape detection except by the medical specialist. Health records are rarely complete. The overactive, aggressive behavior that is a typical result of certain illnesses seems so willful that teachers are inclined to ascribe it to a character defect rather than to its true cause. And as a rule the physical cause, particularly if it is of long standing, is complicated by other conditions, any one of which might itself cause the trouble.

49

In general, physical causes account for a larger percentage of behavior problems in the lower grades than in the upper grades. Partly this is because children do recover under treatment or outgrow handicaps or learn to adjust to them as they grow older. Partly it is because in the course of time the incurables are discovered and hospitalized. But even in high school there are many behavior problems that are due to physical difficulties, and many of these are aggravated by the length of time they have existed.

COMPLICATIONS

Of one boy in Grade I who continually fought other children, couldn't make friends, shouted interruptions in assemblies, and disobeyed all directions, his teacher wrote:

> There are so many possible causes that it's hard to decide on any one. He's repeating and is large for his age. The other children tease him. He's repeating because he missed most of his first year due to a serious attack of scarlet fever from which he almost died. When he was so ill his parents let him do as he pleased. Once convalescent, he began to disrupt the home, and they are now overstrict; for example, when he disobeys they take away his baseball glove for a week. (They pride themselves on never spanking him.) His father is a traveling salesman and rarely home.

Again and again we find that children with physical defects come from homes where, because of poverty, ignorance, low intelligence, or indifference, or all of these, no sustained attempt has been made to secure treatment. Home discipline is often faulty. The mother is likely to be overprotective, the father overstrict, and both inconsistent.

The most pitiful and perhaps the most disastrous complication is rejection of the child by his parents and by other children. Some parents resent spending money for doctors' and hospital bills. Some, frankly or unconsciously, are repelled by a child's looks or by the burden of care. They may threaten the child with being sent away, not for care but to get rid of him. Children, though they can be matter-of-fact in their acceptance of a child who is deformed or weak or who is a stutterer, can be thoughtlessly cruel. Teachers' reports on the handicapped include remarks like: "He's always the last child chosen," and, "The other children won't play with her because she overwhelms them with her loud voice giving orders they cannot understand because of her speech defect." And even high-school students can be callous: "You poor fish—why didn't they throw you back?" If a child's illness has directly or indirectly made him aggressive, such treatment makes him more aggressive still. If he has tended to withdraw, he now shrinks from all contact.

TYPES OF DIFFICULTY

Any illness or deformity or deficiency in development may adversely affect a child's behavior. In some <u>acute conditions</u> like common colds, headache, fatigue, and fever the effect is temporary. Young children's illnesses flare up quickly. A child can be happy and well-behaved one minute and cross the next. If you are alert, you'll often notice an unusual flush or an unusual listlessness. A question or two will let you know whether the child should be encouraged to put his head down on his desk or should be sent to the nurse's room or the office or taken home. Prompt action is essential from the point of view of health, and it may avert a classroom scene. Incidentally, a sick child should not be sent home unless you are sure someone is there to care for him and unless a responsible adult accompanies him.

<u>The aftereffects</u> of some illnesses may include quite specific kinds of behavior. Particularly disruptive is the overactive, aggressive behavior that sometimes, though far from always, follows scarlet fever, measles, diphtheria, sleeping sickness, and some other diseases. The individual is actually unable to keep quiet. He runs, charges violently into others, throws himself about, and attacks other people and their belongings. This behavior is <u>compulsive</u>, that is, entirely beyond voluntary control. But because there is no obvious bodily sign of a serious physical condition, teachers may struggle with a case of this sort for years. We've known cases that disrupted a succession of public and private schools for four or five years before the cause was discovered. <u>Brain injuries</u>, especially those received at birth, may also cause compulsive overactivity. <u>Deficient development of some part of the nervous system</u> may make a child aggressive and overactive. It may also result in mental deficiency. Some authorities now believe a defective central nervous system is associated with <u>schizophrenia</u> in children.

<u>Chronic illnesses</u> take toll in several ways. They may be a direct irritant. They drain the physical resources of the individual. They may upset him emotionally by making him anxious or ashamed. Girls who suffer from <u>leucorrhea</u> (a mucous discharge from the vagina) and boys who have a discharge of pus from the urethra or a bad <u>varicocele</u> (a swollen vein on the testicle) are often afraid to tell anybody. The ordinary school physical examination doesn't disclose the condition. The child feels disgraced and may think he has a venereal disease. Worn out by worry, he may be sullen and cross. <u>Enuresis</u> and <u>lack of bowel control</u> make a child an unpleasant presence in the room and subject him to teasing or rejection. The trouble may be due to laziness or lack of training, but it may be the result of phys-

ical or emotional conditions that leave the child helpless. Acne embarrasses adolescent youngsters and increases their tendency to think the world is against them. Carious teeth and diseased tonsils often go uncorrected for years; the pain and the poisons irritate the child and the accompanying bad breath embarrasses him. The child with chronic heart trouble, asthma, or other chronic illness may feel different because he can't play the games his friends enjoy; and he may be spoiled by the care and attention he must have, and may presume upon his disability.

Deformities also make a child feel different. There's a comforting theory that the physical defect is compensated for by a strength of character. But for one person who, like Franklin Roosevelt, rises superior to his handicap there are many who are overwhelmed.

Malnutrition, whether due to lack of food, to an unbalanced diet, or to an inability to assimilate the required nutritional elements, may cause maladjustment or mental illness.

Small stature, unusual height, obesity—any great departure from the norm of the group—marks the individual. We laugh at the "bantam cock" of a boy, and so do his classmates. But it's not funny to him. The chip on his shoulder is his claim to respect. The outsize of the boy who has repeated one or more grades shames him into bullying. The fat boy has a role to play. He laughs at the kidding, but it hurts. And he seeks comfort in eating more and more.

Speech defects, including stammering and dialect, may subject a child to ridicule by other children. The defect may escape the parents' notice, either because they have similar defects or because they've become used to the child's way of speaking, and thus a condition that could have been prevented or easily corrected becomes chronic. Teasing destroys the child's security. We're struck by the number of reports we have of children with speech defects who shout out in class, "You all hate me," or, "Nobody likes me." The natural reaction of a child like this is to fight everybody. This is healthier than withdrawal, but it's hard on classroom order.

Poor vision and defective hearing handicap a child's learning, and his sense of frustration may make him misbehave. Richard Church, the English poet and novelist, in his autobiography, Over the Bridge (E. P. Dutton & Co., Inc., New York, 1956), has a moving account of his childhood experience with myopia and the miracle that glasses wrought. For his first two years in school he was unable to learn to read, spell, or figure, and was constantly punished for idleness. Church writes of "that dark blur of print below or around the pictures; a blur that tantalised and reproached me now that school had taught me of something concealed in those shadows on the page.... Caning after caning paralysed not only my brain but my nerves.... By the time I had been struggling for two years... I had begun to have frightening dreams, and to wake in the night, sweating so freely that my flannel night-shirts tortured me." Then a school physician discovered the nearsightedness and his parents took him to have glasses fitted. "I remember still the astonishment with which I saw the smaller letters change from a dark blur into separate items of the alphabet." And one evening, two or three weeks later, "when I was sitting at the kitchen table... I looked up at the Swiss clock, in its wooden case on the high shelf over the stove. And I read the time! ...I have remembered the position of the clock-hands ever since. The time was twenty minutes past six."

DIAGNOSIS AND TREATMENT

When considering the possibility that a pupil's disorderly behavior is caused by illness or a physical defect, keep in mind the fact that you are not a physician. Even a psychiatrist, though he is required by law to have a medical degree, generally depends on another physician for the preliminary physical examination of a patient. Though a connection between behavior and a physical condition seems obvious, as in the case of small stature or obesity, there may be other physical factors too. And for you to prescribe any kind of treatment is both unethical and dangerous. Take obesity again. If you tell a child whose obesity is a symptom of glandular trouble what to eat or not to eat, you may be giving him the worst possible advice. Your role is not to diagnose or to prescribe but to do all you can to secure professional help for the child and professional guidance for your handling of the behavior problem.

There is a deep satisfaction in having started the process that leads to the discovery and treatment of a child's physical disability. The effect on his behavior is often prompt. Even if his behavior continues to be bad, the knowledge that it originates in a condition beyond his control makes you sympathetic and objective. And sympathetic, objective treatment may in itself change bad behavior into good behavior. The first step is to study the health record of every child in your room, preferably before the start of school in the autumn, and to restudy the record of any chronic offender.

The health record should make note of everything that might adversely affect the child's constitution or development. Family history as well as personal history should be explored. For example, if there has been color blindness in the family or if the mother had German measles during pregnancy, these facts should be entered. Particular attention should be paid to the possibility that the child suffered a brain injury at birth and to severe accidents and illnesses, though recovery seemed normal. Whenever a doctor has explained the implications of a specific illness or injury for a particular child's learning or behavior, the explanation should be attached to the record. If any of the information about a child is confidential, it can be kept in a separate file, perhaps in the principal's office. In general, however, the teacher is entitled to full information. Of course he must be ethical and not discuss what he knows with people who are not directly concerned in helping the child.

Unfortunately, few schools have even a satisfactory form for the health record, and fewer still make a point of filling out the record completely and keeping it up to date. You will know how far you can trust the records in your school. Even if they are excellent, you should consider the possibility that some physical difficulty has escaped discovery or recording.

The school nurse can be your greatest helper when you are investigating the causes of a child's behavior problems and when you are trying to have them remedied. She has an accumulated knowledge of the child and of his family. She is used to visiting homes and is almost always welcomed by the parents and treated with respect. They readily confide information to the nurse that they might withhold from the teacher or a strange doctor. Her years of "dispensing Band-Aids and sympathy" give her a place in the children's affections, and when a child is suffering an emotional upset he will talk to her and take advice from her. If a special physical examination is indicated, she is probably the school official who will be responsible for arranging it. She may be responsible for seeing that a child who needs continuing treatment reports regularly to the clinic, and she often provides the transportation. This offers her a chance to inspire the child to control his behavior in school. For these reasons, it is well to make a point of knowing your school nurse and of being friends with her. And when she wants your cooperation, for example, in releasing a child from class, give it cheerfully.

Routine school physical examinations vary in quality almost as much as do school health records. Medical authorities agree that a thorough examination every other year is better than a superficial annual examination that takes half the time. The best examining physician is a specialist in the age group of the children whom he is examining. He is thoroughly trained in mental hygiene, and has enough professional knowledge of the symptoms, causes, and treatment of maladjustment in children to decide when an emotionally upset child needs psychiatric treatment. Finally, he understands the school situation, and specifically the difficulties that the teacher of a particular child faces. Such understanding makes his suggestions for helping the child practical; it may make the difference between keeping a child in a class where his maladjustment would be aggravated (and the class continually disrupted) and transferring him to a special class or an institution where his recovery could be rapid. The schedule of examinations should allow the doctor time to explain to the teacher, to parents, and to children who are old enough to understand, the implications that a physical condition has. If there is a probable effect on behavior, this should be described. Time is saved and information made dramatically concrete if a parent and the teacher are both present during the regular examination of younger children. Teen-agers are old enough to assume some responsibility and to take the initiative for correcting their defects. The doctor should have a frank talk with each youngster.

A special physical examination is indicated in the case of a chronic offender whose record fails to show a thorough examination within the year or since the trouble started. The physical cause of a behavior difficulty may develop slowly and the cumulative effect be so gradual that the cause-and-effect connection is far from obvious. On the other hand, the development may be relatively quick, particularly if a child fears or feels ashamed of a condition that he discovers for himself. Therefore, a marked and continuing change for the worse in behavior calls for prompt action. If there is a physical cause, immediate diagnosis and treatment may be the best if not the only hope of correcting the difficulty and of reversing the trend in behavior.

You are lucky if you have a sympathetic, well-trained school physician whose official duties include advising on behavior problems. Generally the school physician is employed only to give routine examinations and does not undertake special examinations except as a favor. The usual procedure is for the principal or the school nurse to ask this favor of the doctor.

Often the only way to secure a special examination is to have the parents take the child to their family physician or to a clinic. The school nurse may be the best person to secure the family's cooperation, though the school principal or you yourself can make the suggestion in a conference with the parents. But our experience, our reports from teachers, and the results of various investigations agree that large numbers of parents fail to provide even minimum medical care for their children.

Health records show how often carious teeth, diseased tonsils, and faulty vision go uncorrected year after year despite strongly worded notices from the school doctor. (Parents who are present at an examination are more likely to take action.) It is hardly to be expected, then, that a novel idea like having a physical examination as a step in correcting misbehavior will impress poor and ignorant parents. They will probably not be willing to spend money for a doctor's fees unless someone like the nurse makes repeated home visits and becomes responsible for appointments.

The doctor who examines a child because of a behavior problem will want a considerable amount of information from you. He may depend on you for facts like date of birth, address, and family background (see "Outline for a Brief Case History," page 46). Your account of the child's behavior is especially important, because the way the child behaves may afford clues to his physical condition. Give as much specific detail as possible. One teacher wrote: "At recess, Nat, aged 10, hurled himself feet first on the back of Clara, aged 8. While I was picking her up to see if she was badly hurt, he dashed 100 feet across the playground, snatched a bat from a big 12-year-old boy and hit him on the head. Another teacher took him to the principal's office. The principal paddled Nat and brought him back to my room. Nat walked down the aisle to his seat, sweeping the books off each desk as he passed. Before I could catch up with him, he launched himself through the air, waving his arms and shouting, 'I'm a bat.'" An account like this means more than the statement, "He's overactive and aggressive."

One word of caution: Don't suggest a diagnosis to the doctor, even indirectly. The doctor may resent your trespass on his province. And there's more than a possibility that you are mistaken.

After the examination the doctor may be willing to confer with you, the principal, the nurse, and other members of the school staff, such as the social worker. A case conference is more satisfactory than the more usual written report, and far, far more satisfactory than a verbal report relayed by the parent or the nurse. Sometimes when you are not sure that you have been given all the information the doctor meant you to have, you can arrange to talk with him privately. But when you talk with a family physician, you must be prepared to have him put all the blame on the school. He naturally supports his patient. And there are still a considerable number of doctors who do not regard teachers as members of "the professional team," even though failure to cooperate with the teacher may have dire results for the patient.

Special examinations of vision and of hearing often disclose defects that are missed in the routine examinations by school doctors, nurses, and physical-education teachers. Eye charts and group audiometers are useful in screening but not a substitute for an examination by a specialist.

PROGRAM ADJUSTMENTS

Experience has shown that some modifications of the regular school program have excellent effects on the behavior of ill and handicapped children. There is rarely any objection to curtailing the program of a child with a defect in vision or of one whose difficulty is obvious. When the only symptom is bad behavior, parents may feel that a child who is excused from a class period is being slighted, and teachers may feel that he is being rewarded. But both parents and teachers welcome any adjustment that brings relief.

Modifications in the regular program include daily rest periods and special lunch periods for children suffering from malnutrition or chronic fatigue, or both. Prolonged breaks in the midmorning and midafternoon may help the compulsively overaggressive child to control himself. When an illness or handicap automatically excludes a child from an activity, e.g., the crippled from games and the epileptic from the use of power tools in the shop, tactful provision of a share in the activity may avoid a behavior difficulty. The classic example is the cripple who keeps score.

The half day, or the quarter day, has already been suggested as a possibility for a maladjusted child. The compulsively aggressive child probably sincerely wants to control his temper and his tendency to run and to fight, and he may succeed for an hour or two or three at a stretch. If he is allowed to attend school for a shortened day and does succeed in behaving well, he gains self-confidence. The period may be lengthened from time to time, but this should not be done until the pattern of good behavior is thoroughly established.

The special class or school (for example, for crippled children, children with speech defects, or children with poor vision) reduces the child's feeling of being different. The other handicapped children and the specially trained teachers treat his difficulties as matters of fact. And the teachers are able to help him learn techniques of adjusting to the everyday world. In some types of difficulty (for example, in extreme compulsive overactivity due to brain injury) the special school run as part of a hospital program is the one slim hope for eventual recovery. When a doctor diagnoses a condition of this kind, prompt

steps must be taken to remove the child from school. To keep
him in school aggravates his difficulties, handicaps the learning of other pupils, and risks his injuring himself and others.

A NOTE ON REPEATING

Experience and research agree that requiring a child to repeat a grade, even if he has been absent for a long period because of illness or has regularly been excused for part of each
day, is seldom advisable. The repeater is likely to be oversized
for his grade and consequently a behavior problem. His attitude
toward learning is usually poor, and he may actually retrogress
during the year. On the other hand, children who, despite their
absences, progress with their age group from grade to grade
may achieve up to grade level or beyond, and generally behave
well. Retardation is recommended only if the pupil is physically
and socially as immature as the majority of the boys and girls
who will be in his class if he is kept back.

CLASSROOM PROCEDURES

If you can build up an ill or handicapped child's feeling of
security, you go a long way toward preventing behavior problems or, if he is already disorderly, toward helping him learn
control. Even when his behavior is compulsive, provided it is
not so extreme that removal from school is necessary, he will
do better in his attempts to manage himself if he feels secure
in your understanding and support.

The essence of emotional security is the feeling of being accepted and valued as oneself and for oneself. In the case of the
ill or handicapped child this feeling must be so strong and sure
that it balances the child's differences from other children, differences that are obvious to him and to them. Your manner and
your actions are important both for their direct effect on the
child and because the other children will follow your example.

When speaking to a handicapped child, try to use the same
tone of voice that you use with the other children. Don't let pity
show. When you are giving assignments, be alert to suggest
something he can do without too great difficulty. Include your
suggestion for him in a series of suggestions to other pupils;
don't single him out by putting him first or last. If the class or
a committee is making plans, let him choose his own part. Let
him try anything that you have any hope he can do, but when he
is overambitious, ask him frankly, "Are you sure you can do
that?" and offer him the choice between two or more possible
parts. When he does a good job, one that would be superior for
any pupil, let him know that it is good. When he surprises you

by doing something you thought he couldn't, something that shows he is advancing in physical or emotional control, praise his progress. But don't be fulsome and don't make him a pet.

Firm and consistent discipline is especially important to the handicapped pupil. The child may presume on his handicap and hit another, safe in the knowledge that the other won't hit him back and not realizing how unpopular his behavior makes him. If you indulge him, you mark him. But if you are firm and consistent in stopping such behavior, you add to the child's security by supporting his efforts to manage himself. His knowledge of what to expect if he loses control will help him retain control.

The other pupils may display a healthy curiosity about, for example, a glass eye or an artificial leg, and, because their curiosity has a tinge of admiration, it helps more than it hurts the handicapped child. Only when their lack of sympathy and imagination leads them to make cruel remarks do you need to take action. Then talk with the class when the handicapped child is absent. We have accounts of successful discussions by first-graders of the problems created by a child with asthma, a severely retarded child, and one given to fits of temper. A fourth-grade group organized itself to help a boy who occasionally flew off the handle and attacked everyone in sight; the four biggest boys in the room would surround him while one girl went for the principal and another for the custodian. High-school home rooms arrange wheel-chair pushers for the crippled and guides for the blind and are astonishingly ingenious in seeing that the handicapped individual never feels left out. When you are talking with your class about behavior difficulties beyond a person's control, lead them to see that, though they must do what they can to help, they must try not to spoil.

CONFERENCES WITH THE PUPIL

A teacher of a difficult 13-year-old, who had had a plate inserted in his skull after an automobile accident, writes: "I make a point of talking with him alone whenever I can, not about his bad behavior, but as a friend. I see him before school, after school, and on the playground. Now he's always courteous to me and is trying to be good, though he still imposes on the other youngsters, who know it would be disastrous if they hit back."

If you take time for repeated conferences with a child who has been ill or is handicapped, he will probably confide in you his compulsive feelings and his fears about the future. You can gradually lead him to see that a great many people in the world have suffered as he has and yet done well with their lives. Let him know that you understand how he feels. Show him that, though he can't control his feelings, he can avoid behavior that hurts others or makes him unpopular. If he thinks he can recognize the danger signs, tell him he is to come sit near you or leave the room when he feels he is about to lose control of himself.

The handicapped pupil is particularly in need of goals and of the security and recognition that come as he makes progress. You can be very helpful here. Read up on his specific difficulty so that you know what favorable developments he can hope for. Study his school record and, if possible, secure an individual psychological examination, so that you can gauge his intellectual possibilities. When you are talking with him, be alert for clues to his particular interests. When you know what he is capable of physically and intellectually and what his interests are, help him set up reasonable educational and vocational goals and intermediate objectives. The a-little-more-each-day approach leads little by little to recovery just as it does in the case of a person who, weak after a long illness, starts by walking across the room, then halfway up the hospital corridor, and then all the way. If you can arrange for the pupil to talk with adults who have overcome similar difficulties, he'll be able to visualize the possibilities. Point out, too, the way President Roosevelt conquered polio and President Eisenhower his heart ailment.

REMEDIAL PROCEDURES

Everything you can legitimately do to speed the physical recovery of a child contributes to improving his behavior not only by adding to his strength but also by convincing him that you care about him and wish to help. A large amount of serious maladjustment and of delinquincy and mental illness can be avoided when the parents and the various specialists (doctor, nurse, speech specialist, physiotherapist) cooperate with the teacher. In this team approach, the teacher's role includes reporting on the child's condition and supervising corrective measures. You can, for example, see that a child eats what he should in the school cafeteria and does the eye, speech, or other exercises recommended by the specialists. Sometimes, if school regulations permit and you are properly insured, you can transport a child to and from a clinic. You may know someone who can be of material help. For example, the Lions Club specializes in helping children with faulty vision, and, if you call the secretary, you can arrange for a child to have an eye examination and be given glasses.

FORCING PARENTAL ACTION

Sometimes when parents persistently ignore the school's advice about proper health care for a youngster, they will listen to the visiting nurse. Procedures for securing her help vary. The school nurse or you yourself may talk the situation over with the visiting nurse or her supervisor. When a family is on relief, the supervisor of welfare is usually willing to bring pressure to bear to have defects corrected. The welfare department is glad to foot the bills. In extreme cases, the Society for Prevention of Cruelty to Children or a similar organization can hale the parents into court. An agency of this type will hold in confidence any information the school gives it. It makes an independent investigation and handles all legal procedures.

STUDY GROUPS FOR PARENTS

More and more schools are taking the initiative in arranging study groups for parents. Health topics are natural subjects for such groups. Most parents are interested in the best diets for children, the prevention of diseases, and the care of children during and after the common childhood illnesses. The discussions should be guided by a pediatrician or nurse. When study groups are part of a PTA program, you might find it interesting and helpful to join one. In any case, you can probably suggest that the group take up problems like spoiling during convalescence (see the excellent advice on the need for firm, consistent discipline during convalescence which Dr. Benjamin Spock gives in The Pocket Book of Baby and Child Care) and the possible aftereffects of children's diseases on behavior.

The school has a special obligation and a great opportunity to promote study groups among parents whose children suffer from a specific illness or defect. Since such a group will generally have to be drawn from all over a city or district, its organization is a responsibility of the central administration. But you can well suggest it, either to your school superintendent or to a parent who is interested enough to take it up with the superintendent. An excellent article in the Journal of Exceptional Children for January, 1949, shows how group meetings of parents of cleft-palate children "foster the kind of professional teamwork in the community that so often is lacking, to the detriment of a total rehabilitation program." When parents of children with speech defects, muscular dystrophy, crippled limbs, or any kind of difficulty meet together, they profit from a kind of group therapy. The knowledge that others share their burden is in itself a comfort, builds security, and helps the parents accept the child. The exchange of information about symptoms and treatment is of practical value and promotes objectivity. Often a group of parents can induce the community to make needed provisions for a special type of child, when a parent or a teacher working alone would be helpless.

POINTS TO REMEMBER

A very large number of disorderly pupils owe their difficulties altogether or partially to the effects of an illness or physical handicap.

The search for a cause of disorderly behavior should always include an examination of the health record and, if possible, a special physical examination by a doctor who understands the school situation.

Some types of illness result in behavior that cannot be managed in the regular classroom. In these cases, early discovery and prompt assignment to a special class or an institution save the child and the school great suffering. Less severe cases may be helped by modifying the school program.

Security and affection are often denied the ill or handicapped child, and the teacher who can provide them wins the child's cooperation. Firm, consistent discipline contributes to security.

Books and Pamphlets to Read

Born That Way, by Earl R. Carlson. The John Day Co., New York, 1941.

Introduction to Exceptional Children, by Harry J. Baker. Revised edition, The Macmillan Company, New York, 1954.

School Health Services, edited by Charles Wilson. National Education Association, Washington, 1954.

(The Journal of Exceptional Children carries authoritative, up-to-date articles on all types of ill and handicapped children.)

Topics for Study and Research

Comparison of a disorderly child and a well-behaved child with the same physical defects. What accounts for the difference?

School and Community Projects

The improvement of special services, e.g., securing a speech specialist on the school staff, a pediatrician with training in mental hygiene as the school doctor, and special classes for children with handicaps.

PTA Meeting

Film: Good Speech for Gary. McGraw-Hill Book Company, Text-Film Department, 330 West 42nd St., New York 36, N. Y.

Topic: Local provisions for the education of the physically handicapped.

VI

Scholastic Misfits

Owen, age 13, Grade VI, IQ 80, has been a failure since he first entered school. Art is the only place he does good work, and there he can only copy. The problem he creates scholastically is dwarfed by the behavior problem which he presents. He delights in molesting younger children. He has a police record of "breaking and entering," and recently was investigated on a morals charge. He steals from his family. Periodic physical examinations have disclosed no defect. His mother and father are both of below-average intelligence. They are both factory workers. The home, which I have visited on occasion, is clean. Owen is always well dressed. The parents have totally disregarded the school's recommendations. Our school has no psychologist or other specialist who might advise me, and Owen's parents refuse to take him to the state clinic in a neighboring city.

—A teacher.

Pat, age 16, Grade IX (freshman in high school), is a member of my poorest English class. He has repeated three grades. The only test result available is a group intelligence test given in first grade. His IQ was then calculated as 94. He talks intelligently but is seldom prepared, and he fails to do as well as boys of less ability because he won't apply himself. He's already been removed from shop class and gym class for lack of cooperation, and is thought to have stolen a teacher's watch. He stammers, but otherwise is reported to be in good physical condition. He has a twin sister, a senior, who is an excellent student and a good citizen.

—A teacher.

One-quarter of the chronic offenders described in our materials from teachers have IQ's of 85 or below or suffer from a reading disability or are two or more years overage for their grades. A good many of those who are retarded have both low IQ's and a reading disability. A few chronic offenders are described as gifted, with IQ's of 130 or above. Pupils who cannot do the regular work of a grade, or who are so bright that the regular work does not interest them, and pupils who are markedly older than their classmates are misfits in their groups. Of course, not all misfits misbehave. Many slow and overage pupils, especially girls, are pleasant and cooperative in the classroom, and the great majority of bright students do good work and are good citizens. But when a disorderly pupil is a misfit, you must consider whether or not his behavior difficulties are due to his academic maladjustment. There are several reasons why they might be.

WHY MISFITS MAY MISBEHAVE

"Frustration causes aggression" is a generally accepted psychological principle. A baby whose arms are held so that he cannot move them will go into a tantrum. He'll thrash around and try every way he can to free himself. Similarly, an older child or adult who finds an obstacle in his path tries to overcome it. If he continues to fail, he may go into a blind rage and attack anything and everyone within reach. The greater the pressure to do the impossible, the greater the chance that frustration will result in such aggression. Some of our most distressing cases are slow students whose parents and teachers have combined in an attempt to force normal achievement.

When aggressive action fails to produce results that please the individual, he may withdraw into a world of fantasy. He substitutes daydreams of success for active effort to obtain success. From the standpoint of mental hygiene, withdrawal is more dangerous than aggression (see Chapter XI).

The desire to conform and the feeling of being different are the two jaws of a vise that may grip a misfit. The very slow, overage, oversize pupil cannot conform and consequently feels forced to justify himself. He's likely to be the class bully. He may become sadistic or use his strength to force smaller boys and girls into sex play. He may steal to gratify some immediate desire of his own or to get money to buy candy for his classmates and thus curry favor with them. And he'll probably join a gang of like-minded youngsters and so gain the security of group membership. The very bright child, on the other hand, is likely to try to hide his brightness by pretending to make as many mistakes as his classmates, and he may misbehave just to prove that he's a regular fellow. Or he may try to gain recognition by concentrating on his studies to the exclusion of all other activities. Being shamed and ridiculed increases any feeling of difference and, therefore, the chances of misbehavior. A slow learner whom his classmates call "dumb bunny" and a bright child who is called "a brain" are alike subject to enormous pressure. If a teacher adds sarcasm, the pressure becomes almost intolerable.

Boredom may be the lot of the slow child because he can't do the classwork, and of the bright child because he does it too easily. Both lose interest in their lessons, and then may wander around, interfere with other children, and generally make nuisances of themselves.

A feeling of insecurity results from the slow learner's experience of failure in his studies. And because he lacks recognition for success in his studies, he sets out, in the classic pattern, to gain attention in other ways. He very soon discovers that 100% failure is almost as noticeable as a mark of 100 and that aggressive misbehavior gives him the center of the stage.

Of course, the fact that a disorderly pupil is a misfit may not be the sole cause of his misbehavior. The slow and retarded often come from poor homes in bad neighborhoods and frequently suffer from physical disabilities.

DETERMINING STATUS

Good cumulative records tell you at a glance if a pupil's age or intelligence is out of line with his classmates'. But good records are rare.

Ages and birth dates are often wrongly given on records. A mistake in this respect may have grave consequences. It distorts test results and leads you to make wrong estimates of relative maturity, intellectual, physical, and social. Therefore, if a pupil is not "behaving his age," you should try to check the record. A telephone call or, better, a note to the registrar of births in the city where he was born is usually all that is necessary.

Standardized tests ought to be given at regular intervals and the results entered in the cumulative record. But there are a great many cases similar to that cited at the beginning of this chapter where the only score available was from a test given in first grade, eleven years before. You must not place much weight on a single test, particularly on one given several years previously. Only if you have the results of two or more tests given in the last two or three years can you feel justified in making deductions from them, and then only if you are sure that the pupil is not suffering from a reading disability.

You must always be on guard against misinterpretation of test results. Notice when the test was given, and compare the pupil's CA at that time with his CA now. Notice whether the norms for the test use the same chronological ages as those in the group tested, and whether the norms depend on the same type of population as that in the group. Norms of a test standardized on children of native white parents are not valid for a class of recent immigrants from Mexico or Puerto Rico. Be sure whether the result is stated as a quotient, a percentile, or a raw score—and when you enter test results on the record remember that some later teacher may be entirely unfamiliar with the test concerned, and be sure to indicate what the results mean. Remember that the older a youngster with an IQ above or below 100 is, the greater is the difference between his CA and MA. A child with IQ 85 has an MA of about 5 when his CA is 6, but an MA of about 13 when his CA is 15. A child with IQ 115 has an MA of about 7 when he is 6, but an MA of about 17 when his CA is 15. The discrepancy is sometimes so startling that whenever you know only the CA and the IQ you should calculate the MA. Change the CA into months, and place the decimal point in the IQ (before the second digit from the right), and then apply the formula CA x IQ = MA. E.g., for 15-year-olds of IQ 85 and 115 respectively, 180 x .85 = 153 (12 years, 9 months); 180 x 1.15 = 207 (17 years, 3 months).

Individual psychological examinations for all children and re-examination on the request of the teacher are the dream of many educators. But very few school systems approach this ideal, and, because of the shortage of trained workers, few can expect to. In fact, the shortage is so great that, even if you work in a system that has a staff psychologist or a working arrangement with a child-guidance clinic, you may have to wait some weeks after referring a pupil for examination before you receive the results and recommendations. In the meantime, if low or high intelligence or a subject-matter disability is a factor in a pupil's misbehavior, you may unwittingly aggravate matters by trying to force him into step with the class. Therefore, in the absence of good records and reliable test results, you should take immediate steps to arrive independently at as objective an opinion as you can.

Your own immediate reaction is a good guide to ability but is not to be trusted completely. You may assume that an overage boy who has repeated a grade or two and is doing poor work for you is below average in intelligence, only to find, when test results are available, that he is average or well above. Psychological examinations of a group of 18 disorderly repeaters revealed that 6 had IQ's ranging from 92 to 118. The remaining 12 ranged from IQ 60 to IQ 87. The poor work that originally caused retardation of the brighter group was presumably due to factors other than intelligence. (In the similar cases in our reports there is frequently evidence of faulty home care or unstable home conditions.) The same factors might well be the main causes of continuing misbehavior. Then retardation would only be an aggravation of the cause, albeit a heavy one.

Low marks, even when they are all a pupil has had over a stretch 'of years, are likewise far from being proof of low intelligence that might be causing misbehavior. The misbehavior

of all chronic offenders, whatever the causes, generally includes unwillingness to study. This and the teacher's feeling of
resentment for a disturber naturally produce low marks even
when intelligence <u>and achievement</u>, as revealed by objective
tests, are above average. On the other hand, we have the "halo
effect": the clean, well-dressed, correctly speaking pupil from
a good family may be thought "surely capable of good work"
when his poor work and bad behavior are actually due to low
ability.

Lacking a record of several tests or an individual psychological examination, you might well give the student some of the
standardized tests that are published for the use of classroom
teachers. These provide methods for determining a pupil's
comparative achievement. Many also contain aids that help you
diagnose a pupil's difficulties. If your system does not provide
standardized tests for your use, you may want to buy some. We
hesitate to suggest that a teacher use his own funds to purchase
such tests, but many teachers who work in penny-saving systems do dip into their own pockets and consider that the money
is well spent. Many publishing houses issue such tests and are
glad to send descriptive catalogues. Most make only a nominal
charge for a sample test, and packages of twenty-five are not
very expensive. Because the companies do not wish tests to
fall into improper hands, you should ask the principal to send
your order on official school stationery.

In giving a test that depends on the pupil's following printed
directions, remember that if he has a reading disability he is at
a serious disadvantage. A pupil whose ability you doubt should
read the directions aloud to you, and you should question him to
be sure that he knows what they mean. Whenever a pupil's
scores on the language sections of a test are decidedly lower
than on the mathematical and other nonverbal sections, you
should investigate the possibility that he has a reading disability.

<u>Objective tests</u> that you make yourself are interesting to
construct and valuable when used. Directions for constructing,
administering, and scoring them are available in most modern
texts on tests and measurements, for example, in <u>Judging
Student Progress</u>, by R. Murray Thomas (Longmans, Green and
Co., New York, 1954). A quicker, simpler, but still illuminating
procedure is to have a student work orally for you. One bright
girl was constantly failing in arithmetic examples that depended
on multiplication. Her teacher knew she knew her tables and
was inclined to blame her for carelessness. Oral working of a
problem showed that the girl was multiplying from the wrong
end.

BASIC PRINCIPLES

Once you have determined that a pupil has a below-average
IQ or is overage, or both, you must accept him as a challenge
to your ability as a teacher. You have to try to adapt the curriculum to him, rather than try to force him to achieve the
norm for your class. You must take him where he is, no matter
how low his level of achievement, and you must not expect him
to make rapid progress. You must pay due regard to his age. A
12-year-old with an IQ of 80 has an MA of 10 years, 3 months.
He may fairly be expected to do the work of Grade V (if he has
no special disability and if he knows the fundamentals up to this
stage), but the ordinary curriculum of the fifth grade may seem
babyish to him. If he is not interested, he will not keep busy.
You must, therefore, find materials similar in content to those
which his chronological age-mates are studying but simple
enough for him to master. We'll come back to this point later,
when we discuss methods and materials.

A slow pupil who is disorderly almost surely has the attitude,
"What's the use? I can't do it, so why try?" He has been frustrated for a long time. To overcome this attitude, you must not
only start him within his range of achievement but accept his
past achievement matter-of-factly. For example, you say, "You
know $2 + 2 = 4$, so you can learn $2 + 3 = 5$," rather than saying,
"You should have learned $2 + 3 = 5$ by now." Having accepted
him at his level, you must exercise all your ingenuity to provide for his making progress that he will be able to see. You
must then praise him whenever you sincerely can—for each
forward step, no matter how short and faltering, and for every
evidence of real effort. He must find satisfaction, i.e., recognition, in doing his schoolwork or he will rebel against it.

The work required of a slow learner should be as closely
related as possible to his actual interests and to realistic
goals. You must, then, establish the kind of friendly relations
that will let you discuss with him his plans for the future. What
does he want to do? How will his schoolwork fit into his plan?
Slow learners are human beings and, like many of us, given to
exaggerating the possibilities of life. The boy who cannot do
simple arithmetic may nonetheless fancy that he will be an air-
plane pilot. He doesn't consider, or else brushes aside, the fact
that a pilot has to be a good mathematician. You'll be tempted
to use his ambition to spur him into harder work on his arithmetic. This is all right if you are sure he can learn the mathematics a pilot must know. If he can't, you are unforgivably
compounding and prolonging his frustration. If he cannot learn
the mathematics he would need, you should, without belittling

him, try to direct his attention to some job related to aviation that he can do.

A knowledge of a pupil's assets is essential if you are to provide him with chances to earn recognition and if you are going to help him establish realistic goals. When we urge teachers who are suffering from a pupil's disorderliness to list his assets, the first reaction is likely to be a flat "He hasn't any." But reflection usually provides a few, and sometimes many— he can draw, or he is neat, or strong, or he coordinates well. It may be that all you can say is, "He's not as bad at drawing as he is in reading." Knowing even that helps you help him. When listing assets, don't confine yourself to the strictly academic. Include physical condition, athletic skills, manual skills, human relations, and character traits like cheerfulness and persistence.

In general, slow learners do relatively better with simple, concrete ideas and materials than they do with the complicated and abstract. This does not mean that they are automatically "good with their hands" and can become skilled mechanics. It does mean that they do better when working with their hands than when working with books. Give the slow learner all the opportunity you can to see and feel and manipulate. Let him use blocks to learn to count. Let him build scenery as his part of a project.

The very bright pupil needs treatment which is the reverse of that for the slow learner. He needs to be challenged to do his best, to do work ahead of what he has done. His program should be enriched by requiring him to do advanced work in the regular subjects and by adding subjects, for example, a foreign language in elementary school and a course from another curriculum in high school. At the same time, he needs careful supervision to see that he doesn't substitute verbal glibness for hard work on the fundamentals.

But when all is said and done, the secret of preventing misbehavior, whether the pupil is dull or bright, is to keep him busy and interested. You can't do one without doing the other.

PLACEMENT

A third-grade teacher in a New York suburb reports a class of 15 girls and 17 boys. Their IQ's range from 76 to 149, their ages from 7 years, 6 months, to 11 years, 10 months. A medium-sized city system has 980 high-school juniors (Grade XI). Their ages, as of January 1, range from a low of 14 years, 11 months, to a high of over 19 years. The median is 16 years, 7 months. There are more than 100 students one or more years older than the median, and 30 students one or more years younger.

Ranges like these are typical of most classrooms in the United States. Obviously teachers do teach pupils of widely different ages and abilities in groups together. But the fact remains that a large percentage of the overage pupils are behavior problems. Therefore, if you have an overage disorderly pupil in your room, you should certainly consider trying to have him placed in a higher grade where most of the pupils are as old as he is.

Transfer to a higher grade is particularly recommended when objective tests indicate that the overage pupil's intelligence is in the average range, and most particularly when they show that his achievement (without regard to his marks) equals the actual achievement (as distinct from grade norm) of a fair number of the pupils in the higher grade. Such "promotions" have been shown by experience to result in great changes for the better in behavior and in learning. The transferred pupil is relieved of the need to misbehave and of the opportunity to abuse younger children. Of course, the teacher in the upper grade should be willing to take him as he is, but even if the curriculum is not adjusted to individual differences, the pupil will be no worse off than some of his new companions are. Therefore, although the teacher of the upper grade may accuse you of trying to get rid of a troublemaker, be persistent when you are sure of your ground. The reverse procedure, retarding or demoting a pupil as a punishment for misbehavior, is a crime against the future, because he will surely behave worse.

Placement in a special class for the mentally retarded, when one with an appropriate age range is available, is indicated for most pupils of IQ 75 or below. When such a student finds himself in a class where his limitations are accepted and the curriculum is gauged to his ability, there is a better chance of his behaving well. And even if he is not helped, the regular class is relieved of a very difficult problem, which the special-class teacher is trained to handle.

Formerly, special classes existed only in elementary schools and the pupils left school before they reached high-school age. The increased years of compulsory education have resulted in the retention in school of many mentally retarded boys and girls of 15 or 16 or older. They are too old to mix with elementary-school children, and the tendency is to place them in the freshman or sophomore class of high school.

If a secondary school is going to have to provide for mentally retarded pupils, they should certainly be grouped together. Those who are able can share shop, gym, art, and music with the regular classes and in many ways share the life of the school. But they should not be allowed to remain in regular academic classes, where they inevitably lower standards and are at best a burden and too often a disruptive force.

In the case of the very bright pupil who is a behavior problem, one of the first moves should be to give him work that is interesting and challenging. If this cannot be done in his present grade, careful consideration should be given to placing him in the next higher grade immediately or having him skip a grade at the end of the year. If by any chance he is overage for his present grade, he might well be put ahead by two grades. In general, a youngster who is accelerated should have an IQ above the median IQ of the class into which he moves. His achievement, as tested by standardized tests, should be above the average of the higher class in every subject. He should be physically and socially mature enough to hold his own with older children. A psychologist reports:

Dorothy was referred for examination because she was failing her work in November of her second year in third grade and was a constant troublemaker in class. She proved to have an IQ of 150 (Stanford-Binet). Achievement-test scores placed her reading at sixth-grade level and her arithmetic at high fifth-grade level. Investigation showed that she had been able to read before she entered first grade. She'd always been something of a problem behaviorwise, and during her first year in third grade spent more time in the principal's office than in her classroom. It was recommended that she be tried out in fifth grade, and she was moved ahead immediately. A routine follow-up in January found Dorothy well-adjusted. She was at the top of her class, happy, and well liked by her teacher and her classmates.

Sometimes a secondary-school student is disorderly and uncooperative because the course he is taking does not fit his interests and needs. Our materials contain several cases of disorderly boys who are enrolled in the college course though there is no chance of their going to college (they are neither acceptable students nor top-flight football players) and though they are wasting their own time and that of their teachers and classmates. Some of these boys actually want to go to trade school. Others, with skillful guidance, might see how the general course or the business course would prepare them for an occupation they would like. Similarly, there are boys in the general course who might more profitably be in a business or vocational-trade course. In all of these cases, the best hope of changing the student's behavior is to put him where he can see that his schoolwork is preparing him for an occupation. Unfortunately there are many boys (and not a few girls) for whom no suitable courses are ordinarily available. To dump these on the trade school or, in desperation, assign them to the general course does no good.

When a school does not offer a course of interest to a student and when he won't work, or at least behave himself, in the most suitable course available, there is great doubt whether staying in school beyond the legal leaving age does not do him more harm than good. Certainly he is no asset to the school. Under these circumstances teachers, guidance officials, and principal should do everything they can, including getting him a job, to arrange his withdrawal. When the school is sure it is right, it should insist on withdrawal.

The difficulty in forcing withdrawal or in shifting a pupil to another class (except to advance him to be with his age group) is generally the opposition of the parents. They may be over-ambitious for their child or unable to face what they consider a disgrace. They may blame the teachers and appeal to the school board. But if you are patient and willing to keep trying to show the parents how the change may benefit their child, you will succeed in overcoming the opposition in a large number of cases, particularly if you have the active cooperation of a guidance counselor, your principal, and, not least, the pupil himself.

In talking with parents you should point out some specific good qualities that the pupil has, especially when a change of course would let him capitalize these and obtain employment in the future. And remember how much you help parents by just listening patiently and sympathetically.

METHODS AND MATERIALS

The slow or bright student may continue to be a problem no matter how well he is placed if you do not adapt to his abilities the materials and methods that you use. There are several pamphlets and a great many books that offer practical advice; for example, Reaching the Mentally Retarded, by Jack W. Birch and Godfrey D. Stevens (Public School Publishing Co., Bloomington, Ill., 1955), and our book Teaching the Bright and Gifted (Prentice-Hall, Inc., Englewood Cliffs, N. J., 1957). The Gifted Student as Future Scientist, by Paul F. Brandwein (Harcourt, Brace and Company, New York, 1955), has broader implications for secondary-school discipline than the title indicates.

The first necessity, after you are sure of a pupil's level of achievement, is to discover his interests. The gifted child may be interested in a wide range of subjects at the adult level. The slow learner generally has the same interests as his age-mates. If you are used to talking with youngsters about what they do out of school and what they hope to do in life, you have a good start. Requiring your class to write essays on the topics, "What I like most to do out of school," "The subjects I

like best," "My major problem at home," and "My major
problem in school" will produce many clues. The slow learners
may not write fluently but may still turn in very revealing papers. If a student's ability to write is so poor that he is inhib-
ited from any expression of opinion, try having him talk to you
about the topic. Sometimes you can discover the interests of an
uncommunicative pupil by talking with the other members of the
group when he is not present. "What does_____like to do?"
is a natural question. However you obtain clues, develop them
in the series of conferences recommended earlier.

If a student belongs to any kind of club (for example, the
Boys' Club), the director or a club worker may be able to give
you valuable information. You'll find that club officials are well
aware of the youngster's difficulties in school and will be eager
to give you help if you ask for it.

Certain goals should be, and generally are, shared by all
adolescents. These include knowing how to keep themselves and
their clothes clean and their clothes "in style," what kinds of
food to eat to be sure of a balanced diet, how to care for themselves and others during simple illnesses, how to handle cash,
the rights and duties of a jobholder, how to make simple home
repairs, the ordinary rules of etiquette, the basic requirements
of happy marriage, and the fine points of several sports.

If you will keep these goals in mind and analyze the possibilities of promoting them within the broad framework of your instruction, you will find that there are many times when you can
cater to the slow learner without holding back the average or
bright student. Then, in your conferences with the slow learner,
try to help him understand how he can learn things in your
class that will contribute to the goals we have mentioned. If he
can see some usefulness in school, half your battle for better
behavior is won. Etiquette is of concern even to the most unruly, and you may give much-wanted help to a disorderly student when you show him parallels between correct classroom
behavior and correct adult manners.

You can teach more, and the slow learner can learn more, if
you are using methods that allow a student to work at his own
speed on materials he can understand. But the subject matter
must be of interest to him at his stage of social development.
One teacher, who found a 16-year-old could read only at the
fourth-grade level, gave him a fourth-grade workbook. The boy
was quiet for a period or two while he enjoyed the novelty of
being able to understand something from a printed page, but he
quickly reverted to bad behavior. Indians did not interest him.

Gateways to Readable Books: An Annotated List of Books in
Many Fields for Adolescents Who Find Reading Difficult, by

Ruth Strang and Others (H. W. Wilson & Co., New York, 1952), and Reading Is Fun, A Graded List for Reluctant Readers. by P. G. Matthews and H. Pardue (Library Journal, 62 West 45th St., New York 36, N.Y., 1953), will help you match materials to both interest and ability. School and public librarians can also give you, and your students, excellent advice about easy books that appeal to older students. If your class is going to the library, tip off the librarian about the interests and relative abilities of troublesome students. They may accept from the librarian suggestions about reading that, coming from you, would be suspect as "more work."

You will certainly try to help the slow learner make all the academic progress he can, but you must be realistic about both the extent of learning and the kind of learning that are possible. Slow learners not only learn less than their brighter agemates, but also stop developing earlier. Secondary-school teachers in particular should remember that the 15-16-17-year-old slow learners may not now or ever be capable of doing more than sixth-grade work, no matter how hard and how long they try. For example, they can be trained to use simple arithmetic in buying and selling, but they'll never be able to grasp abstractions like $(a+b)^2$.

Reading presents special difficulties for many students. Some secondary-school students who are about to leave school still need to be taught to read street signs and labels in shops. (They will probably have a knowledge of figures adequate for reading prices.) These are extreme cases. But many need intensive help in learning to read directions, the newspaper, and magazines. A little extra help will show many that reading is fun and start them on the habit of reading magazines and books for recreation. If you try to force such students through a curriculum of the classics, you get nowhere. But if you can show a student both the desirability and the possibility of attaining a goal that you know to be within his range, you may find that he'll stop wandering around and interfering with others and settle down to work.

If your school has remedial reading teachers and other special teachers, they can help you diagnose difficulties and provide extra instruction. With or without expert help, if you are using a method that permits students to work as individuals, you can arrange for a bright student to give some help to a slow learner. Parents also can help. But you have to be very sure that student helpers and parents understand the limitations of the slow learner and the best methods to use with him. Otherwise they may push him too hard and thus add antagonism to frustration. They may also make fun of his mistakes, and this is fatal. The safeguard is to set up a program with definitely prescribed materials and periods. When you ask one student to help another, the brighter should understand and agree that the tutoring gives him a better understanding and knowledge of the fundamentals. He should not have to sacrifice much time that he might better use in enriching his own knowledge. The slower should have some opportunity to share with the brighter in other activities, e.g., chores and games, in which the slower is not at a disadvantage.

Sometimes two relatively slow students can work at lessons and at chores together. The feeling of equality gives both of them security, and they encourage each other to do better. You may be afraid that they will become partners in crime, but they are more likely to exert joint effort toward improvement.

Slow learners get more out of films and other visual-education materials than they do out of books. They won't see as much in a film as brighter students do, but they may very well see enough to hold their own in the class discussion. This helps them feel more like regular members of the group and thus reduces the chances that they will try to upset the group.

The importance of creating this feeling of worthy group membership can hardly be overemphasized. You will be repaid for all the ingenuity and effort you expend to promote the feeling. Praising any good contribution is the means, but you have to stimulate the contributions in some way. If you use a unit or project method of instruction, try to be extra sure that the slow learner has a part he can play that the group will recognize as helpful.

BUILDING RESPONSIBILITY

Just because slow learners cannot excel in academic work, they respond well to being assigned classroom chores and other nonacademic duties. Many such duties they can do as well as anyone, and duties against which brighter pupils might rebel as being dull or repetitious the slow pupils welcome. You must, however, be careful not to humiliate the slow learner or distinguish him from the group by always assigning to him the more menial tasks. Duties are best rotated, unless (as is possible in high school) they are paid jobs, like working in the school cafeteria. If a chore requires more ability than a slow learner has, let him share it with a brighter friend.

When you find that a slow learner does a particular job well, lead him gently to see that he might later find satisfactory employment in work of this type. If you can help him obtain part-time paid work along the same line, do. Earning money of his own gives a youngster intense satisfaction. It keeps him from getting into trouble out of school, and if you are instrumental in getting a youngster a job, he'll feel sure that you like him and want to help him. And that is what he needs.

POINTS TO REMEMBER

Work that is too hard or too easy may cause misbehavior.

Standardized tests of intelligence and achievement are essential as checks on teachers' opinions.

Individual psychological examinations of all children are desirable.

Curriculum and methods should be adapted to individual differences in ability and achievement.

A pupil's own interests can be used to motivate better work.

Retardation is always dangerous and generally futile. It should never be resorted to as a punishment.

Special classes for the mentally retarded have proved their worth. There is need for more special classes in both elementary and secondary schools.

Acceleration is desirable when a pupil's intelligence and achievement qualify him to do the work of a higher grade and when he is socially mature enough to hold his own with older boys and girls.

Books and Pamphlets to Read

Adapting the Secondary-School Program to the Needs of Youth, National Society for the Study of Education, Fifty-Second Yearbook, Part I. University of Chicago Press, Chicago, 1953.

Educating the Retarded Child, by Samuel A. Kirk and G. Orville Johnson. Houghton Mifflin Company, Boston, 1951.

The Education of Exceptional Children, National Society for the Study of Education, Forty-Ninth Yearbook, Part II. University of Chicago Press, Chicago, 1950.

Topics for Study and Research

Why do pupils with the same IQ sometimes differ so markedly in achievement and behavior?

The effects of retardation (and acceleration) on achievement and behavior.

What develops persistence?

What materials and methods are useful to catch interest, give responsibility, and otherwise help the disorderly slow pupil to learn?

School and Community Projects

Psychological service by qualified school psychologists.

Remedial teachers.

Special classes for mentally retarded boys and girls at all levels.

Diversified high-school curricula.

PTA Meeting

Film: Problem of Pupil Adjustment—The Drop-out; The Stay-in. McGraw-Hill Book Company, Text-Film Department, 330 West 42nd St., New York 36, N.Y.

Topic: How parents can help with homework.

TEACHING THE DISORDERLY PUPIL

VII

Faulty Home Care

Quincy, age 6, Grade I, was a discipline problem in kindergarten. Last year he was in the reading-readiness group and spent most of the year out of the room because, when present, he kept the class in an uproar. Teachers, principal, psychologist, and school social worker have been collaborating in an attempt to improve matters. We found that his father and mother did not seem interested in him, but only in his three younger sisters. The father would bring home toys to the girls, but not to him. They let him run wild, and then strapped him if a neighbor complained. The teachers have gone all out to be patient and extra kind and to carry out the psychologist's recommendation about matching work to ability. The principal has tried to reason with him when it was necessary to have him in the office, and whenever he has done something nice the teachers send him to the office for praise. The social worker has managed to change the parents' attitude. They now give Quincy as many toys and as much attention and praise as they do the other children. The father no longer straps Quincy but talks with him. Both parents come to PTA meetings. Quincy has shown slow but definite improvement in school, and his conduct out of school has improved somewhat. The long line of complaints has broken. We're hopeful about next year.

—A teacher.

Ralph, age 13, Grade VIII, is the pet topic of conversation of all the teachers who have ever had him. I'm often greeted, "How are you getting along with the school wrecker?" He's defiant, impertinent, a bully, and given to sexy remarks. He dresses flashily. He's always bringing teachers expensive gifts. (Bribes?) When I tried to contact the parents I found they run a bar and restaurant. Both work there from 10 a.m. to 1:30 a.m. They're making money and convinced that's the best thing they can do for Ralph. They're asleep when he leaves for school. He gets his breakfast from "the woman upstairs," and his other meals at the restaurant. This has been going on for six years. All that time he has been hanging around corners with a bad gang.

—A teacher.

Sam, age 17, a high-school senior, wants to leave home. He says he can get into the Navy and his parents will be glad to see him go. He has been in trouble in school, but he is bright and I've persuaded him to work for his diploma. I've tried to show him that his parents are having a hard time bringing up six children—he's the oldest—and that he can't blame them for being tired and cross, especially when his behavior adds to their troubles.

—A teacher.

In whatever neighborhood you teach, you are sure to have some pupils who are handicapped by faulty home care. Three-

79

quarters of the teachers who have given us reports on individual chronic offenders state that the home environment is at least a contributing cause of the child's difficulty. These teachers represent all grades and every type of community. The 4,270 teachers whose opinions on behavior were included in the 1955-56 NEA survey put irresponsible parents first as a cause of difficulty, unsatisfactory home conditions (low wages, broken families, bad housing), second, and lack of parental supervision due to the mother's working, third.

The conditions some children face in their homes are so burdensome and of such long standing that you can be forgiven if you think there is nothing you can do about them. This feeling of despair is acute when you have a large class of underprivileged children and realize how many public agencies have worked with their families and failed. What can you, without specialized training in social work and without legal backing, do in a few hours a week during a few weeks in the year?

YOUTH IS RESILIENT

First, you must reassure yourself by remembering that the vast majority of such children do rise superior to a bad environment. Usually you have only to think of the brothers and sisters of a chronic offender from a bad home to realize that not all the eggs in the basket are rotten. And you can take courage from reports like the following:

The one and only discipline problem in my third grade this year is Tim. He is a big boy, old for the grade (a repeater), and overweight besides. He came into my room not seeming to care about anything or anybody. Papers were never finished and sometimes not even started. He was always talking, fooling around, and upsetting class routine. I never could get him to take part in any of the games, but he was always trying to disrupt them. At recess, during lunch period, whenever the children were on the playground, someone would come running to me complaining about Tim's bad behavior. When told to do something, Tim's answer was a silent refusal. He and I had a couple of sessions in which the law was laid down pure and simple. It seemed to work for a day or two, but then he'd go back to his old ways. One day Tim turned in a fairly good paper so I asked him if he would like to take it home to his mother. "Oh, she doesn't care. She's never home. Nobody cares." By further questioning I discovered that the mother spends all day at the family restaurant helping her husband. She works nights, too, and Tim is left in the care of his high-school-age sister. He is pretty much on his own most of the time, doing as he pleases, and with no one to care one way or another. After learning this, I tried to spend more time each day with Tim, talking to him, encouraging him in his work, and showing him that the class and I cared very much about his work and his marks. I got the school psychologist to test Tim and found his IQ is 97. He could do the work, and gradually as he tried harder he did better and began to concentrate on finishing all assigned work on time. We didn't stress his lack of participation at game time. For a couple of weeks he watched the others silently, but without interfering. Then, slowly, he began to stand with the group. Finally, one day, he actually played a game with us. I believe his clumsiness and his "nobody cares" held him back. After realizing that we all cared and wanted him to join the fun he took an active part. From then on, his behavior in the classroom and on the playground was all right. But the home problem was not solved. The principal and I are trying to get the parents to come to school so that we can talk with them about Tim's need for supervision, love, and encouragement. They've promised to come, and perhaps we can bring about a change in the home, too.

In cases like this, you have to exercise all your skill as a teacher and you need all the proverbial patience of your profession. But if you can find out what is wrong at home, you can do much to supply the child's physical and emotional lacks. You may be able to secure the cooperation of the parents in correcting home conditions. When the parents cannot or will not cooperate, you may be able to secure outside help to force them into a new pattern or to place the child in a better environment. You can't expect success in every case, and you can't expect quick improvement. But experience has shown that boys and girls do respond when they see efforts are being made in their behalf, and that a very little assistance from you often gives them the extra strength they need to overcome obstacles.

TYPES OF DIFFICULTY

In this chapter we are confining our discussion to children in homes where both parents are present. In most of these cases the parents could give the children better care. The mistakes under these circumstances center around poor discipline, favoritism ("sibling rivalry"), and neglect. In addition, parents who are down on their luck may blame a child for the expense and trouble he causes, and thus add rejection to his other burdens.

Neglect is most frequently caused by both parents' working at paid jobs so that neither has time to give a child proper amounts of love, attention, and supervision. Other causes of neglect are poverty, overcrowding in the home, and ignorance.

The simplest, most direct evidences of neglect are dirtiness unusual for the pupil's age, inadequate, uncared-for clothing, uncorrected physical defects, e.g., carious teeth, and sheer starvation. When you can remedy material deficiencies like these, you'll often see an immediate change for the better in the pupil's behavior. A first-grade teacher reports:

Urban was my discipline problem child. He is one of fourteen children, nine of whom are in school. The family is very poor. He sleeps in the bed with a brother and two sisters. They have no indoor plumbing in their house. I had to ask an older brother to teach him to use a flush toilet. He was constantly annoying other children by spitting on them, pinching them, and lifting up the girls' dresses. When I talked to him about his behavior he began to cry. I found through the weeks that standing near him, giving him jobs to do for me, and letting him be leader and praising him when he did well were good weapons. I know he doesn't have any hot water at home, and he comes to school with dirty clothes and a dirty body. So I've begged clothes for him and I've arranged with the janitor to let Urban bathe in a sink in the basement with a sponge I gave him. Urban now takes great pride in showing me how clean he is. He says, "I love you next best to my mother." He's no longer a problem. In fact, he keeps reminding me of this: "I'm doing good for you, huh, Miss Sundy?"

If neglect produced only material damage, there would be few resulting behavioral difficulties. But the psychological damage of neglect, and even more of faulty discipline and of mismanaged sibling rivalry, is profound. The child feels deprived of love. He is insecure. He feels inferior, either to a sib or to the other pupils in the room, or to both. If he is of tough basic fiber, he may assert a precocious independence and substitute a neighborhood gang for his family. If he is unable to develop emotional strength independently or with the aid of a teacher or some other adult outside the family, he may show the scars of his struggle throughout life. Children of families in all walks of life suffer from faulty discipline, sibling rivalry, and feelings of being unwanted.

PATTERNS OF BEHAVIOR

You can almost never be sure of diagnosing the cause of a disciplinary problem from the specific ways in which a child behaves. Most of those who have been deprived of legitimate means of satisfying their needs for affection, security, and recognition react aggressively. They are almost all attention-seekers. They talk out or, as one teacher says, "talk parallel." They wander around the classroom. They clown.

There are, however, a few cause-and-effect relationships that occur frequently enough for you to consider them first when a given kind of behavior is present. There is some evidence that children who are crowded in with their parents and siblings of the opposite sex are inclined to initiate sex play in school. The insecure child may steal to be able to treat other children and thus buy standing with the group. The severely dominated child, especially if the domination takes the form of beatings, may be sullen and inclined to withdrawal. The spoiled child tries to be the center of attention and to boss the other children. But, on the other hand, a spoiled child may be afraid of other children and withdraw, and the dominated child may show a healthy tendency to fight back. Of one boy who "seems to explode every so often, does exactly as he pleases, and is continually fighting," his teacher says, "There seems to be a direct relationship between the way he is treated at home and the way he acts in school. The more he is punished at home, the more difficult he becomes in school."

CAUSE AND EFFECT

Though two pupils may misbehave in the same ways, your plans for helping them should be based on a knowledge of what is causing their difficulties. The child who "talks parallel" because he is spoiled at home and has to have his own way may learn better if you and the other pupils ignore his plays for attention. The talker who is trying to force attention or to disrupt the class because he resents the way he is being treated at home is most likely to behave better if you give him lots of attention and praise; instead of ignoring him you have to set up opportunities for him to work with and for you. Moreover, knowing why a child behaves as he does leads you to think about what you can do to change conditions and so puts a stop to the blind recrimination between home and school which often complicates efforts to build up the child's power to overcome adverse influences. When his parents and teachers blame each other, he may blame both and be sure that neither can help him.

You have to be on your guard against jumping to conclusions about conditions in a home. If you are familiar with the neighborhood from which your pupils come, you quickly associate the pupil's address with the type of home found on his street. You may be tempted to assume that a boy or girl from a good address is spoiled by wealth and that one from a slum is the victim of poverty or neglect, though your common sense and your daily contacts with other children from the same streets will convince you, if you stop to think, that wise and loving care of children is not confined to middle-class homes. You must, too, beware of prejudice of any kind. Teachers in general are remarkably free of racial and religious prejudice; they may not be so tolerant of customs that differ from their own. One teacher, after visiting the home of a pupil, was sure that the child would come to a bad end: "Why, they expected me to drink a cup of wine!" Another wrote: "I don't see how Vic will ever amount to much. His family has a butler and a lot of servants. I was served tea in a real Lowestoft cup."

You can reason yourself out of your own mistaken ideas but still let yourself be misled by the prejudices of others. You want all the information other teachers can give you about the parents of the pupils you teach and about home conditions. But their opinions may be swayed by their own prejudices, and even

more by unfortunate experiences they may have had with uncooperative parents. Nurses who visit homes regularly, trained
social workers, and pastors are more reliable sources of
information. In the last analysis, however, there is no completely
satisfactory substitute for firsthand contacts with the parents
themselves. You may make these by visiting your pupils' homes
and by inviting the parents to come to school for conferences.
The latter is the more usual procedure. But a conference, especially a conference over a problem of discipline, is far more
efficacious if friendly relations have already been established
by a visit in the home. Moreover, many parents find it practically
impossible to visit school in the hours when a teacher can be
free for a private talk. Such parents are doubly appreciative of
being sought out.

HOME VISITS

The ideal system is for every teacher to be given time to
visit the home of every child whom he teaches (or, in the case
of the secondary-school teacher, the homes of students in his
home room), so that pupils and parents regard it as routine.
Some systems manage to do this. One method is to pay a substitute while the teacher makes his visits. Another method is to
pay the teachers extra to make the school census, and to plan
the census so that each teacher visits the homes of the pupils
in his room. This is sometimes done in the week before school
opens. Where there are large families, such census taking by
teachers results in some duplication, but it is a simple matter
for the teachers to arrange who is to ask the census questions.

In most systems, however, the teacher who visits homes does
so on his own responsibility and on his own time. Allowing a
half-hour visit in each place and time to get from house to
house, visiting the thirty or more homes may take thirty or
forty hours. The question is, is it worth it? Teachers who make
visiting a regular practice reply, "Emphatically, yes!" They
say that it does more than anything else to establish a warm
friendly atmosphere in their rooms. If you visit your pupils'
homes, they are convinced that you are interested in them.
They take pride in showing you where they live. The parents,
who always hear enough about you to be curious about the
strange sun around whom their children revolve day after day,
welcome the chance to meet and talk with you. They feel that,
if you are willing to take the trouble to come to their home,
you are surely doing everything you can to help their child in
school.

The first visit or two may present something of a mental
hazard, particularly if you are to visit parents whose racial or

economic background is strange to you. But a few cordial welcomes will dissipate this. You'll be offered all kinds of esoteric things to eat, drink, and smoke. You need not accept any of these—a simple statement that you are making several calls will explain your abstinence—but if you are courageously curious, you'll gather many a new and delicious recipe.

You can reduce your feelings of doubt about home visiting and be sure of finding a parent at home if you will explain to your class that you expect to visit every home and ask them to talk with their mothers and invite you to come at a time that will be convenient. This always produces several invitations, and by the time the word gets around that you are visiting, you'll find that practically every family will invite you. If you are not invited, you can either ask for a specific invitation or take a chance and drop in. It's a good plan to take with you a pupil's paper on which he has done well, or at least be prepared to describe something about him or his work that you particularly like. If you start with praise, the subsequent conversation will take care of itself. It doesn't have to be, and shouldn't be, limited to the pupil and his activities. The main purpose of the home visit is to establish friendly relations. You will naturally acquire a great deal of information in the process. Make yourself a friend first and you will be in a good position to ask questions about background if the need arises. But if the pupil or his parent offers to show you where he studies, his hobby shop, and his books, be sure to accept.

You do not have to ask questions or pry in order to garner information. Parents like to talk about their children. If you listen and look, you will fill in many gaps in your knowledge of the youngster. The case of a boy who seemed to have no special interests, who always wanted to lead but did nothing to show leadership, and who was constantly distracting the class by talking and inattention is described by one teacher:

His mother had often visited the school. I knew already that she was nervous, that she talked in his presence about how Winston increased her nervousness, and that she always brought him to school in her car though other children from that neighborhood walked. I visited the home and found that it was well appointed and spacious, that Winston has a large accumulation of toys, which he hoards but doesn't play with much, that he keeps his room in unnaturally good order, that his parents buy him everything he wants. The situation is complicated by the grandparents' sharing of the house. The four adults work together managing a shop a few blocks from the house. Winston is often left alone. He is not allowed to play with any of the children in the neighborhood. I had thought he was just spoiled. I see now that he is overprotected and that I shall have to work towards getting the family to let him live the way other children do and learn to play and share with them.

In the case of another child, who doesn't know how to play with children and is "forever fighting because he loses his temper when he cannot have his own way," the teacher found out, when he visited the home, that "Xavier's older brother has a serious eye disease which has necessitated several operations. Through all this time, the parents have neglected Xavier. They began to realize this as they talked to me. I hope it isn't too late."

Try to avoid letting the child hear his parents criticize him to you. They may do this even if they are overprotecting him. Overprotection is sometimes compensation for feelings of guilt. The parents may feel guilty because they reject the child or because they resent the trouble and expense he causes. But when they talk with you the underlying rejection and resentment emerge in the form of criticism. Whatever the circumstances, the child who hears his parents and teacher talk over his shortcomings has his feeling of being unwanted confirmed. The way to stop a parent who begins to criticize a child is to ask a distracting question about some possible interest of the parent's or about something as commonplace as the weather. The principle of diversion is as useful in controlling adult conversation as it is in controlling child behavior.

It hardly seems necessary to warn you about gossiping. But parents who know that you are visiting several homes in the neighborhood may give in to their natural curiosity. If you respond, you are almost sure to be misquoted and you may make enemies.

You may not be able to visit every home, but you will find yourself amply repaid for the time and effort involved in visiting the homes of all your troublesome pupils. One teacher who is famous for his ability to handle the worst sort of problem says:

I'd no more think of trying to help a difficult boy without visiting his home than I would of starting on a complicated motor trip without a map. In all of my experience I haven't found anything else as helpful as getting to know the parents in their own home. They give me leads on how to help the boy. They're quite sure, though often inadvertently, to give me clues on why he behaves as he does. And sooner or later they and I together manage to work out changes in the way he is treated at home which help change his fundamental attitude.

CONFERENCES WITH PARENTS OF A MISBEHAVING PUPIL

Unfortunately the first time most teachers meet the parents of a chronic offender is when the parents are summoned to school to discuss his misbehavior and to plan ways in which the school and home can cooperate. The parents are on the defensive and may be in a combative mood. The teacher may feel desperate and inclined to blame the home for everything. But, if the interview is handled carefully, these handicaps can be overcome. In any case, the procedure is a necessary one. You have to be sure that parents, including fathers, know that their child is not behaving well in school. Your responsibility is limited and temporary. Theirs is complete, in both the moral and legal spheres, and permanent. Notes home and telephone calls do not discharge your obligation to keep the parents posted. Both notes and calls may miscarry, and neither give you the information you need or the chance to take constructive action.

When you are going to talk with parents in school, try to ensure privacy and try to arrange a time when there is no hurry. There should be adult-sized chairs for everyone—a minor detail that is too often overlooked. Start the interview by letting the parents know that you realize it is inconvenient for them to have to come to school, and thank them for making the effort. Make it clear that you want to help them help their youngster. You can do this by stating the case not as a complaint but as a problem: for example, "I've been wondering how we can help Yates learn to study instead of wasting his time." Soften your account of misbehavior by mentioning any favorable things about the youngster that you possibly can.

Be a good listener. Parents who are given a chance to talk profit from unburdening themselves and may arrive at solutions that would be resented if you suggested them. The parents may be full of complaints about the school. Let them get these off their minds. Only if a complaint is based on a lie by the pupil, and then only if it might affect future actions, need you defend yourself. For example, younger children who suffer from a urinary or bowel difficulty which should have medical attention frequently blame their "accidents" on not being allowed to leave the room, though you have given them permission to go to the toilet whenever they wish. Older students may claim that all their study periods have been taken up by doing something for you, when you know that they have been fooling away their time. In cases like these, say that you think you and the pupil had better talk the matter over with the parents present. Just the idea that you will do this usually results in the truth's coming to light, or at least in the complaint's being dropped. Children also frequently lie about what happens at home, and use imaginary episodes as excuses for not doing their work and for being late or being absent. Again, the sure means of straightening matters out is for all concerned to meet together.

A conference with a parent should lead to some definite and constructive suggestions for changes in the way the child is treated at home and for future home-school cooperation. When a parent makes a suggestion of which you approve, be quick to single it out. Break in with, "I think that suggestion of yours that you should invite the neighbors' children to play in your yard is very important." Emphasis on the fact that an idea is the parent's and that you approve assures its being carried out. If no constructive suggestion is forthcoming from the parent, don't hesitate to make some of your own. You must be tactful and you shouldn't be radical. For example, you can hardly insist that a mother give up her job, but you can ask, "Is there any way that Zeke could have a hot lunch at noon?" One caution is necessary. Do not encourage parents' suggestions that they punish a child at home for the way he behaves in school. In particular, discourage corporal punishment by the parents for school offenses. This is very different from encouraging firm, consistent control of a spoiled child. It is different too from suggesting that a student who neglects his homework should not be allowed to go to the movies or have dates on weekday nights, at least until after his work is done. If you advise or even approve of home punishment for behavior like talking and fighting in school, the pupil believes that you are his enemy and that the whole world is against him. But if he knows that you have vetoed additional punishment, he may be grateful enough to try to cooperate with you.

A teacher of an unruly fourth-grader writes:

I arranged a conference with Andy's mother and followed with another conference with her two weeks later. Then I met with his father. In the meantime I had several talks with Andy. Little by little I worked out what I thought ought to be done and got the parents to agree (1) to arrange for Andy to play with boys his own age instead of with younger boys and with girls; (2) to stop comparing Andy with his older sister who does so much better than he does in school; (3) to praise his accomplishments; (4) to give him chores that had to be done daily; (5) to be consistent as to what was to be punished, and that each parent would be firm about not letting him do anything that both had agreed he should not do.

THE COOPERATIVE PARENT

Most of the parents of your pupils are eager to work with you for the good of their child. But in the case of a chronic offender there is a considerable chance that something has gone wrong in the home environment. When there is something wrong in the home, the parents are often unwilling to cooperate. Some of them are afraid to face their own mistakes. Others are so absorbed in their own troubles, financial or emotional or social, that they cannot apply themselves to their children's troubles. You can tell very quickly. The cooperative parent keeps his appointments and makes a sincere effort to carry out what he has agreed to do, whether this is taking the child to a clinic or seeing that he does his homework every night.

When a parent is willing to work with you, you have to estimate as carefully as you can both the parent's intelligence and his emotional frame of mind. The bright parent who treats his child's troubles with objectivity and, when the occasion allows, with a sense of humor is able to explore with you the possible causes of trouble and to discuss the child's background in some detail. A parent like this might profit from going over with you the outline for a case history that appears in Chapter IV. The emotional worrier, on the other hand, might become very much upset if you asked a direct question—about whether the mother had had German measles during pregnancy, for example. And if the mother was ignorant, she might remember all the old-wives' tales about the dire effects of a pregnant woman's seeing a black cat. So watch your step, and remember that parents will usually of their own accord pour out their troubles in a way that will give you all the information you need.

BOOKS FOR PARENTS

As a teacher, you are used to learning from books, and you may be tempted to think you can solve your problem by recommending a book or pamphlet to the parents. As a matter of fact, few parents, even well-educated ones, read nearly as much as authors and experts would like to believe. True, the distribution of the excellent government pamphlets Your Child from 1 to 6 and Your Child from 6 to 12 has been phenomenal. The famous and important books by Gesell and Spock have long been best sellers. But if sales are compared with the number of families who have children in the corresponding age groups, it is evident that relatively few families bring up their children "by the book." Moreover, many parents who own books on child care do not read them. We've had the amusingly distresssing experience of being asked to autograph a book whose pages were still stuck together though the parent said it had been bought a year previously. And again and again, when we recommend a book, a parent will say, "I own that but I've never read it."

Nonetheless you should be familiar with the standard books for parents. The government pamphlets are cheap and can be obtained through a bookseller or direct from the Government Printing Office, Washington, D. C. Spock's books, Your Baby's First Year and The Pocket Book of Baby and Child Care, are available in paperback editions for 35¢ and can be found in most drugstores. The books from the Gesell Institute, by Arnold Gesell, Frances L. Ilg, and Louise B. Ames, now cover the development of children through adolescence. The titles are Infant and Child in the Culture of Today, The Child from Five

to Ten, and Youth—The Years from Ten to Sixteen. Ilg and
Ames have also written a useful book, Child Behavior, which is
now available in a paperback edition. Parents who face problems of discipline in the home (including sibling rivalry) might
be helped by our Better Home Discipline. Parents who tend to
spoil and overprotect a child or who have an only child might
read our The Only Child. Dominating parents might try New
Ways in Discipline, by Dorothy W. Baruch. Most of these books
are available in public libraries, and all of them can be ordered
through any bookstore, but don't be surprised if you have to
give the parents the name and address of the local store. Parents
who would never read a full-length book might find help in our
two brief pamphlets, You Were Young Once, Too and The Age
of Decision—How to Help Your Teen-ager, which are available
for 10¢ from the Mercer Publishing Company, 22 East 52nd
St., New York 22, N. Y.

TACT AND TACTICS

Your experience with hundreds of children and your professional knowledge of child behavior justify your giving a great
deal of direct advice to parents. As we have said, this is most
likely to be accepted if it comes in the form of confirming a
parental suggestion. On the other hand, if you initiate a positive
suggestion, you may be met with the remark, "But you have
no children of your own. You can't understand." Parents
rarely consider that the experienced teacher deals every day
with more children the age of theirs than the parents can
possibly have. There's no point in arguing with a parent. Having
made the suggestion, you have to count on its sinking in and
coming out later as the parent's own idea.

When parents are worried by some type of behavior that you
know is usual for a given age, you can help them greatly. Parents rarely remember the way they felt and acted as teen-
agers, much less as nine-year-olds. If you can reassure them
that there is nothing fundamentally or permanently wrong with
a child, that he is behaving just as thousands of other children
behave, you may give them a sense of security that will clear
the emotional atmosphere of the home. At least you can help
them ignore the normal while they work on a problem that is
significant.

Parents who have children with similar problems profit from
group discussions in PTA meetings and from study groups like
those described in the chapter on handicapped children. The
difficulty is to find a qualified leader. The school may employ
a psychologist or social worker who can organize and conduct
groups. Or a local or state child-guidance clinic may set up

discussion groups under the guidance of a leader who is trained in group therapy. Sometimes a teacher or principal has the background and the necessary common sense. Keep posted on groups which are meeting, and keep in mind the possibility of suggesting to the proper authorities that new groups might be formed.

FATHERS ARE PARENTS, TOO

The typical American father looks on child rearing as a woman's business. He gladly turns his sons and daughters over to his wife and to women teachers, without thinking that every child needs a good adult model to learn how men should behave. Your visits to a home are likely to be in the afternoon, when the father is away at work. Similarly, conferences in school come at hours when it is very inconvenient for the father to be there. Though he might be cooperative if the need were firmly impressed upon him, he too often doesn't come into the picture until it is too late.

Fathers make many mistakes that may affect their children's behavior in school. Some fathers are too busy to pay much attention to a child and may actually repel the advances the child makes. A man who is tired from a long day in the office naturally wants to settle back in his own overstuffed armchair and read the paper. When he drops into the chair and lands on a pair of skates, he can be forgiven for losing his temper. When he is reading an account of a football game and has just got to the point of deciding what play he would have called and how it would have won the game, he doesn't want to stop and answer a question about arithmetic. Fathers are major violators of the principles of discipline. They are often overstrict and dominating and inclined to inflict severe punishments, including severe corporal punishment. But they are often inconsistent, particularly about backing up their wives when a child appeals from a penalty or deliberately does something which both the child and the father know the mother disapproves. Finally, fathers as well as mothers may favor one child over another and so increase the danger of sibling rivalry.

A library could be filled with books that give good advice to fathers. In addition to the general books listed earlier, the studious father might be helped by Fathers Are Parents Too, by O. Spurgeon English and Constance J. Foster. If you have the opportunity to advise a father, there are a few simple recommendations that you should try to impress upon him. He should be sure to make opportunity to express his love for each child and his pride in that child. He should arrange to spend some time alone with each child each week doing things the child likes to do with him. When he is playing with a child, the play should be with him and not for him—the child should have the major part in building a block tower or setting up an electric railroad. If the child is working with his father in the garden or at a hobby, he should have a project of his own. It's very much better to watch for seeds to sprout when you've planted them yourself than to spend time watering seeds your father has planted; it's better to sandpaper the hull of a boat model you have made than to stand by while your father finishes a table top and hand him a fresh sheet of sandpaper when he asks for it.

Fathers should arrange for children to visit them at their place of work. This helps the child fill in the gap of absence by thinking of what his father is doing. Moreover, the father's colleagues, whether they are laborers or lawyers, are sure to be nice to the young visitor and to speak highly of the father, and both contribute to the child's pride in his parent and thus to his security. The father is often the best person to take a youngster and his friends on trips and excursions, to the museum of science, to a big-league ball game in New York, or to fish in a near or distant stream. Here you may be the instrument of fortune, since there are many trips children can take in connection with their schoolwork and you can suggest to a father a specific place where he might take his youngsters.

Older boys are in special need of tactful handling and support from their fathers. The boys are in the stage when they are declaring their independence. The fathers realize that the boys will soon have to hold down jobs. But they may clash over how irresponsible the boy seems at the moment and over what the boy wants to do. We shall come back to this in the chapter on the unruly teens. The principle involved is to help the boy explore possibilities for his future education and employment, but also to encourage him to make his own decisions.

THE NONCOOPERATIVE PARENT

You will find that a great many parents of chronic offenders are virtually inaccessible. They do not come to school when invited. They do not answer letters. If they have phones, they hang up on you when you call. And if you do succeed in talking with them, they may say that the way the child behaves in school is all the school's fault. A few will show active animosity toward you and the school. One father told his son's teacher: "I hated school and left as soon as I could. The teachers always had it in for me. I wouldn't have Bob in school except the truant officer is always on my neck. I hope he raises hell." But most noncooperation can be traced to ignorance or to the parents' being absorbed in their own problems.

When parents fail to appear for a conference, some principals write them that their child is suspended until they do come. We know of enough cases where boys have intercepted letters of this kind, or have themselves answered telephone calls and pretended to be the father, to make us think that this is a very dangerous procedure. The boy then runs wild, and almost surely gets into serious trouble with the police before anyone knows what is happening. In contrast, if you persist in trying to see the parents in their home or manage to find one at his place of employment, the very fact that you have tried so hard to see them may produce favorable results. One way of making contact with a parent and bringing pressure on him at the same time is to work through his employer. This seems a harsh step to take, because there may be danger of damaging the employee's standing with his employer. As a matter of fact, we've found most employers more than cooperative. Many take an interest in seeing that the father talks with you and that he carries out your recommendations. Some take constructive steps to help the child and the family when they realize that things are not going as well as they should. And a few companies maintain social-service departments which are designed to help employees and their families keep out of trouble.

WORKING WITH FAMILY AGENCIES

When you cannot secure parental cooperation or when you are sure that a family problem exists which cannot be solved by the family with what help you can give, you should try to see that some social agency accepts responsibility for the case. This is not always easy. There is a tremendous shortage of trained social workers. Public as well as private agencies are loath to increase their case loads. Many rural communities and small cities have no casework agency of any kind. Your first task, then, is to be familiar with the possibilities and to know the steps in referral. When you cannot find an agency willing to take over and the situation seems serious enough to warrant strenuous measures, you can suggest to your principal that the matter be referred to the local probate court. The judge of probate has power to force parents to care for their children, and to commit neglected children to the custody of the state.

When a social agency is working on a case that involves a child in your room, suggest to the worker that you and your principal be invited to sit in on a case conference about the child. This should be routine procedure, but the pressure on case workers is so great that they sometimes neglect it. If you attend a conference of the doctor, the psychiatrist, the social worker, and the welfare department's representative, you will find that you will learn much which will help you manage the child constructively while he is in your room. You will find, too, that you have much to contribute which will help the other workers understand the child's problems. This is particularly true if, in their concern about the parents' troubles, they are not giving the child's feelings due consideration. The members of a case conference will be especially grateful if you can present a brief but specific anecdotal record of a child's behavior over a period of a week or two.

The fact that a social agency can frequently help you solve a difficult school problem indicates that you should take an active part in one of the agencies in your town. Almost every agency is organized as a society, with members who hold meetings. The main purpose may seem to be to raise money to support the agency's work, but that's another reason why you should be a member. The dues won't be high, and when the Community Chest drive comes around, you'll feel happier about working for the Chest and contributing to it if you have a personal interest in a particular agency. (Of course, a large amount of the money raised by the Community Chest is for the benefit of children. The Chest deserves your active support whether or not you are a member of one of the participating agencies.) Well-organized family societies generally have at least one teacher on their board of directors. If you are asked to be a board member, try to accept. The work is interesting and rewarding. Moreover, if as a member of a society or as a board member you know the director of an agency, the personal contact helps you get quick attention for a case when you think there is need. Even if your agency does not handle the kind of case you face, the director will know who should be called and will more than probably be willing to relieve you of the details.

SUPPLYING DEFICIENCIES

When you know or suspect that a certain type of difficulty in the home is causing a pupil to misbehave in school you can supplement the shotgun attack we described earlier by specific measures aimed at supplying deficiencies. You can also be extra careful to avoid actions that might make matters worse. We have touched on some of the implications for the school that are inherent in specific conditions. You will find many things you can do if you will use sympathetic imagination in considering the home conditions of a chronic offender. In general, you can do a great deal to correct the results of neglect by seeing that the pupil has proper clothes, a chance to clean up, proper food (a quart of milk a day is a big addition to a deficient diet), and a chance to make up lost sleep. One teacher reports: "Eleanor's father and mother have periodic drinking bouts, and, when one is on, the children are kept awake all night. I can tell by looking at her when she comes in whether she's had sleep or not. If not, I have her put her head down on her desk and nap for an hour. This makes an enormous difference in her behavior through the rest of the morning."

You will of course do what you can to convince each pupil that you like him for himself no matter how bad his behavior may be, and you will try to see that he has chances to earn favorable recognition from you and his classmates. Don't forget that if he has a goal which he is trying to reach, and that if he and the class have a group objective to which he can contribute, he will try hard to do his part and the other pupils will recognize not only his efforts to help but also the fact that he is no longer interfering with their plans and work.

The emotionally upset child who is worried by what he sees at home or by the way his parents feel about him or he feels about them profits from a chance to express his feelings. You can lend a sympathetic ear and show your understanding without indicating approval of his feelings or his behavior. One third-grader said of his older sister, "I'd like to take her under the porch and cut her to pieces." Though he obviously meant it, his teacher didn't show either shock or amusement. Instead, the teacher said, "I know just how you feel. I had an older brother who used to make me so mad that I wanted to kill him. But you know, now we're grown up he does lots of nice things for me."

You probably have not the technical training required to direct play or dramatics with a view to helping a child work out a particular emotional problem. Therapy is best left to specialists, and you should avoid amateur interpretation of the drawings, paintings, and compositions of your pupils. But this is no reason for not giving them ample opportunity to work out their feelings in these ways. Try to be sure that all of your pupils have a chance to express themselves creatively in art, writing, drama, and dancing, and that when they show some talent they are helped to cultivate it. In the ordinary classroom the benefit of these activities lies in the activity itself and not in the information that the pupil's behavior might convey to the expert.

Reading and seeing plays and movies are not usually thought of as a means of releasing pent-up feelings, but the individual who becomes absorbed in the story of a hero or heroine in fiction, a play, or a biography experiences what Aristotle called an emotional catharsis. He shares the character's experiences and so purges himself of his unexpressed feelings. You need not try to match the conditions faced by a hero to the conditions you think a pupil faces. The appeal of the classics, of the books that stand the test of time whether they are children's stories like Winnie-the-Pooh or dramas like Oedipus Rex, is universal. They deal with the feelings all of us have whether we know it or not. Try to steer upset youngsters to the famous books that have been enjoyed by boys and girls in their age range.

Some home conditions suggest specific countermeasures that you can take in school while doing what you can to see that the parents change the ways in which they treat the child.

The dominated child needs many opportunities to learn to work on his own. He also needs to learn to lead, both in games on the playground and in classroom discussions and study groups. In brief, he should be given practice in exercising independent responsibility.

The spoiled child needs to learn that attention has to be earned instead of being accorded on demand, that he must not indulge his whims and desires when these conflict with the rights of others, and that unless he waits his turn and does his share he may be denied the very things he wishes. The indicated treatment is for both class and teacher to ignore impulsive and selfish behavior, while praising any effort toward a worthy goal. Routine aids the spoiled child, partly by teaching him that there is a time and place for everything, and partly by giving him a feeling of security. You must remember that the child who is overprotected has little chance to stand on his own feet and that when he is faced with the competition of a roomful of boys and girls he may be frightened into the behavior we associate with spoiling.

Inconsistent discipline in the home must be countered by firmness and consistency in school. The need is not for many rules and regulations to be obeyed unquestioningly, but for understanding that there are some types of behavior that are always unacceptable. The child who has been treated inconsistently may, like the spoiled child, feel very insecure, and a frame of routine gives him support. As a matter of fact, parents who complain about a child's bad behavior at home are often puzzled and surprised at how well he behaves in school. One famous judge confessed to his son's teacher that he could not control the boy at home. How did the teacher do it in school? The teacher had never thought about it, but finally concluded,

"All of my students know that there are certain things I always expect of each and every one of them. They always do them. There is really no problem." In other words, the teacher was friendly, fair, and firm.

Sibling rivalry is a major factor in much misbehavior in school and in much subsequent unhappiness and maladjustment in adult life. Don't be misled by a pupil's telling you how fond and proud he is of the new baby at home. This may be just a way of sharing some of the attention that he sees showered on the baby. Don't be scandalized by extreme statements. Of one boy who was always attacking other children, his teacher writes: "He confided in me that he hoped the baby expected soon would die so his older sister could use the baby clothes for her doll." Let the child have his say. And whenever you have a pupil who has brothers and sisters, try to build him up in what interests and abilities he has that differ from theirs. He may be in desperate need of being somebody in his own right and not just a pale copy of another child. Above all, refrain from invidious comparisons. Very often you will know that your present pupil's behavior and work are far inferior to a sibling's. The temptation to point to his sib's superiority, to make the better student a model, is almost irresistible. But you must withstand the temptation. Only by treating your pupil as an individual with his own claims on your interest and liking can you help him to behave as he should.

POINTS TO REMEMBER

Don't prejudge a child from a bad home. The great majority of children succeed somehow in rising superior to a bad environment.

Don't jump to conclusions about home conditions on the basis of an address or from hearsay. Visits to the home and conferences with the parents are the surest sources of information.

Let parents talk to you. You accomplish more by listening than by giving advice.

Include fathers in your conferences with parents.

Cooperate with social-work agencies. Seek an agency's help when parents refuse to care for a child properly.

Plan your work with a child to remedy the deficiencies from which he suffers at home.

Books and Pamphlets to Read

Better Home Discipline, by Norma E. Cutts and Nicholas Moseley. Appleton-Century-Crofts, New York, 1952.

Fathers Are Parents Too, by O. Spurgeon English, M.D., and Constance J. Foster. G. P. Putnam's Sons, New York, 1953.

New Ways in Discipline, by Dorothy W. Baruch. McGraw-Hill Book Company, New York, 1949.

Teacher-Parent Interviews, by Grace Langdon and Irving W. Stout. Prentice-Hall, Inc., Englewood Cliffs, N. J., 1954.

Topics for Study and Research

Case studies to determine what, if any, relation there is between different types of home discipline and behavior in school and in later life.

Comparisons of well-behaved and badly behaved children from the same neighborhoods or from the same families to discover the determining influences in home and school.

School and Community Projects

A school social worker.

A community social-work clearinghouse that will coordinate information and efforts in cases where families need guidance or material help. The schools should be represented.

PTA Meeting

Films: The Child in the Middle [between parent and teacher]. University of California at Los Angeles. Overdependency. National Film Board of Canada, available from McGraw-Hill Book Company, Text-Film Department, 330 West 42nd St., New York 36, N. Y. Sibling Relations (two films). Mental Health Board, 166 East 38th St., New York 16, N. Y.

Topic: Better home discipline.

VIII

Cracked and Broken Homes

There are 28 pupils, 14 boys and 14 girls, in my room. Eight of these, including a pair of twins, come from broken homes. Of the eight: one teases and hits others, is excessively talkative, and makes dramatic plays for attention; one behaves well, but cannot distinguish fact from fiction; one is quiet but, despite an average IQ, does no schoolwork; one is very immature; one, IQ 117, does very poor schoolwork; one talks a great deal, but children like him and he can be led to conform; the twins are very well adjusted and very good students.

—A teacher.

Florence first came to our school and my room last fall. In two weeks she made 25 enemies. Her mother had died when Florence was 4. Florence spent a year in an orphanage, and then was placed in a series of foster homes — three in three years before her present home, and each change involved a change of schools. Her IQ is 114, and she averages above grade in all achievement tests, despite her moves. I immediately went to see her new foster mother and also asked help from our principal, the state social worker, and the school nurse. All of us have worked together, and in two months Florence has shown marked improvement. She now has two good friends in the class, and no enemies. Her present foster family love her and plan to adopt her. There are 6 other children from broken homes in my class of 26: four in one family, living with their own mother and stepfather, and two living with divorced mothers. All are well behaved.

—A teacher.

Carl, age 16, a high-school sophomore, suddenly began to get into trouble three years ago and has gone from bad to worse since. Investigation disclosed that his parents were divorced when he was 5. He lived with his mother, but saw his father every week. Four years ago his father remarried and had a child. Carl apparently resented the advent of his half brother and the corresponding slacking off of his father's interest.

—A teacher.

More than a quarter of the children in the United States lose the care of one or both of their own parents. Death of a parent is the principal cause of loss, followed in order by desertion and divorce. In addition, there are large numbers of illegitimate children and even larger numbers of children who are deprived of proper love and care because of an alcoholic or a physically

99

or mentally ill parent. In many of these cases the loss is mitigated by the wisdom of the parent who continues to care for the child. A loving foster parent, a stepparent, an adoptive parent, or a temporary foster parent often fills the place vacated by a child's own parent. But in too many cases the growing child lacks the love and security he needs for normal development. He is like a man floundering in quicksand. His struggles sink him deeper and deeper, and he is doomed if someone does not extend him support and show him how to win free.

When parents fail, the child's best hope of support is in you, his teacher. You are probably the only responsible person who sees enough of him to sustain him through his difficulties. If you, too, fail him, he is left to struggle alone in a morass of uncertainty.

SYMPATHETIC UNDERSTANDING

A child who is distressed by the conditions in his home often seems incorrigible in school. His resentment at his situation shows itself in hostility toward his classmates and his teacher. His insecurity makes him seek attention and try to dominate. As a result, he behaves in ways that may turn his teacher and the pupils against him, and thus prevent his earning the love and recognition he urgently needs. Teachers' accounts of children from broken and cracked homes again and again employ the following words: hits, pulls, pushes, fights, punches, bullies; sullen, sulky, stubborn, impudent; yells, interrupts, noisy; blames others, alibis, tattles; lies, steals; bites nails, masturbates, enuretic.

Your success in helping a child from a cracked or broken home overcome his difficulties and change his behavior will depend on the extent to which you feel with him and understand him. Sympathy and understanding will give you the determination and the courage to help the child. And, as he senses your attitude, he will begin to feel that he is wanted.

If you know the facts of a case, you are almost sure to feel sympathy, and there is generally no difficulty in discovering the facts. Most records show the marital status of a child's parents, or at least changes in names. As a rule, the youngsters themselves talk freely: a 7-year-old boy says of his father, "He's a drunk. He hits my mother. He bangs me around. I hate him." Parents, too, are surprisingly frank. For example, a teacher went to see the mother of an 8-year-old boy who had arrived at school dressed in a 3-year-old brother's clothes and with welts on his arms and back. He had said that both were punishments for not having prepared his brother's breakfast on time. The mother said, with the boy there: "He was a mistake—a brat. Now I'm married and we have three real children. I don't see why they should go without for his sake. We want to send him over the hill [to the county home]." Information is often available from other teachers or staff members. A high-school teacher, investigating the background of a boy who was "antagonistic, profane, obscene, and generally uncooperative," was told by a school social worker: "The boy found his own father hanging from a transom. The body was still warm. The mother remarried—a man who had several children by a previous marriage and wasn't interested in this boy. The stepfather is now unemployed. The family has just been evicted from their tenement. A stepbrother is in prison for arson. The mother is a chronic invalid—bedridden, when they have a bed."

TWO CAUTIONS

The attention-demanding behavior of the pupil who suffers from home conditions like these sometimes provokes a scolding. The scolding, however, exacerbates his feelings of being unloved and insecure and may make him behave all the worse. A third-grade teacher writes: "David is one of many placed-out children from a large broken family. He has red hair and a low IQ and feels 'different.' When I scolded him for pushing in line, he yelled at me, 'You're a monkey.'" A high-school teacher writes: "Grace's parents were divorced when she was 9. She never sees her father and has no desire to do so, though he lives near. One day, when she was particularly antagonistic, ignored my instructions, and walked away when I was talking with her, I became angry, told her to sit down, and to apologize. She cursed me and walked away."

If you stop to think of the problems that a pupil from a poor home faces, you will be inclined to be as gentle as you can in what you say to control him. You may have to speak very firmly, but you can still speak in a low voice and be polite. If you can bring yourself to say, "Please be quiet," you may be surprised by a spontaneous apology. But if you yell, "Now stop pushing. And apologize to Harriet," you convince the offender that you are against him, and you smother any hope he may have of your ever supporting him.

Ignoring, which is so useful in controlling the attention-seeking behavior of the spoiled child, has limitations as a method of control in the case of children from broken homes. Unless recognition for worth-while activities accompanies ignoring their misbehavior, their insecurity drives them to compel attention at any price. A teacher writes:

Ida is a little girl in my third grade. Her mother is divorced and remarried. Ida has been in 7 schools in 3 years. She persistently interrupted the class by calling out, "My pencil broke," "Oh, hum, I'm tired," "Shut up, I can't work," and similar expostulations. She fought with all the children so much that they stopped speaking to her. They called her "the pest." The children and I decided to ignore her. She got worse and worse and finally took to running out of my room into other teachers' rooms and calling them names. The principal got in touch with Ida's mother, who said she was very surprised. Ida, she said, loved school and insisted on coming even in the worst weather. The principal had a heart-to-heart talk with Ida and her mother, and then one with Ida alone. He convinced Ida that she had to "tend to business" if she were to be allowed to stay in school, and threatened to suspend her for a week if she didn't reform. This was not an idle threat—we'd made up our minds that we had to have a respite. Ida, who apparently really does love school and likes me, understood. She's improved steadily ever since, and I've been able to do much more with her and for her.

CONSTRUCTIVE ACTION

An analysis of teachers' accounts of their treatment of children from broken homes reveals three generally successful techniques. The pupils respond to frequent friendly talks with the teacher. They profit from being praised for schoolwork that they have done well and for chores that they have done for the teacher. They seem to be specially helped when the teacher is able to maneuver them into leadership of a group activity.

Talks with you give the child an opportunity to unburden himself. His parents may be so emotionally upset themselves or so antagonistic to the child that they never let him talk things out with them. He is left uncertain about all of their plans. If he knows that a separation is impending or that a parent is gravely ill, he wonders what is going to happen to him. Who is going to feed him, to see that he has a place to sleep? If you can gain his confidence, if you can let him talk and talk, you can do much to reassure him. You may actually know what the plans for him are and be able to convince him that he will not suffer. You may be able to find out what his ambitions are and make detailed plans with him as to how he can fulfill them despite the situation at home. At least you can point out that many other children have found themselves in the same sort of situation and have survived happily. One teacher writes: "I let him talk with me before school in the morning, at recess on the playground, before school at noon, and then walk home with me. Very effective!"

Your praise helps the child who needs love and recognition, not only by raising him in his own self-esteem but also by raising him in the esteem of his fellows. If the other pupils hear you praise a chronic offender, they begin to believe that he cannot be all bad. In telling of the boy who was allowed to talk to him before and after school, the teacher says: "He obviously resented others' having things he did not have. My efforts to help him go on every day. I give him something extra to do. He does little chores, washes boards, empties the basket, and has charge of the paint cups. I praise him for his trivial accomplishments. Now he really tries to be courteous to me. And the other pupils are beginning to be willing to play with him." Asking a student to help you is in itself a form of praise because the request shows your confidence in him. In the case of the high-school boy cited at the beginning of this chapter, whose bad record went back to the time when his father remarried and had a new baby, his teacher writes: "I have got him interested in being an audio-visual projectionist for me. His attitude in class has changed since then. For the first time, he has actually obeyed me and has cooperated to the extent of doing his homework."

A second-grade teacher kept a running diary of the behavior of one 7-year-old girl. Here are a few excerpts that show the good effects of chores and of praise.

> I asked Jane if she behaved that way at home. She blurted out, "I ain't got no mother." I find that her mother ran away with another man. She lives with her father and grandmother. The children in the neighborhood are always taunting her with, "You ain't got no mother." . . . I asked Jane if she'd like to be flower monitor. She beamed and smiled with joy. Today her work showed marked improvement. . . . Yesterday I sent a good paper home to J's grandmother. Today she announced, "Grandmother says I'll soon be upstairs with the big people!" She tapped her pencil only once and stopped when I smiled at her. . . . We've discovered Jane needs glasses. I've changed her seat to the one next the board. She is quite pleased with herself—and so, less tapping. . . . Jane turned her back on the flag during flag salute. I ignored it. Next day she did it again. I took her gently by the shoulders and turned her around. She's not done it again since. . . . The glasses came, and Jane announced, "I'm going to work like second grade." But she spent all day taking her glasses off and playing with them. I talked to her and pointed out that I have to wear glasses, too, and that I keep mine on all the time. . . . A month later—Jane is trying to "work like second grade." She's making progress, and I'm showing her that she is, and helping her to evaluate it. Most of all, I'm trying to give her lots of my affection to make up in some small way for the loss of her mother's love.

The good effects of making a pupil a leader stem from the recognition the group gives him and from the security he feels as an accepted member of the group, a member who has something to contribute. Three typical cases follow.

> Earl, Grade VII, changed from a fair student, who was looked up to by the other students for his athletic ability, into an interrupter and aimless wanderer who did no work. I found out that his mother was seriously ill in the hospital. I went to see her. She obviously expected to die, and was very afraid

of how Earl's father, a very strict disciplinarian, would treat him. She said she guessed Earl knew how she felt. After a talk with him in which I pointed out that an athlete had to be a good student if he was going to be a smart ball player, I moved Earl up from the middle reading group to the top group. At first he was overawed. We talked together, and he agreed he had to enter group discussions. Within two weeks he began to express his views and was very careful to follow the "rules of courtesy" set up by the group. He took his turns as group leader and found that he had to prove himself as good a leader as the others. His behavior at school and at home is now fine. The home problems aren't solved, but they are lessened by Earl's improved behavior.

The day school opened, Fred, Grade V, lost no time in showing me that he was not only a poor student but also a clown. He would never answer a question asked of him, but would bellow out the answers to questions asked of others—or rather, his idea of the answers. During seat work he was always noisy. He would pretend he was a train, repeating over and over, "Choo-choo! — Choo-choo!" When reprimanded, he'd stop temporarily and then begin the same sound all over again. The school social worker came to me and explained his background. His mother had divorced his father, who was a drunkard and used to beat up his wife and children. She has remarried, but unfortunately Fred's stepfather makes no secret of his dislike for him and whips him for the way he treats other children in the neighborhood. The social worker said that Fred needed a firm hand in discipline but, at the same time, lots of recognition and affection. The first response I got from him came when I praised a paper. It wasn't much in content, but it was neat. Ever since, he has kept his papers neat and tried to improve their content. The greatest change came when I let Fred be a leader in athletic games and group work. He has slowly learned to make friendly and acceptable advances to the other children, and to accept or reject their suggestions politely.

The class has sincerely tried to help Glenn, Grade III, become a better member of the group. In spite of the way he had treated them, they choose him to work on their committees and praise him for the excellent work which he does. He responds well for a few days to the praise and then relapses again. But the intervals between relapses are lengthening out.

WORKING WITH PARENTS

From time to time you will probably have to work with parents who are in the process of getting divorced, parents who are already divorced, parents left alone by death or desertion, stepparents, foster parents of adopted children, and foster parents of placed-out children. The books and pamphlets listed at the end of this chapter will help you deal with such parents and will help them give their children proper care.

Parents who are in the process of breaking up their marriage are not usually in a mood to accept advice. And you are not in a position to give it. You are not a marriage counselor, and amateur attempts to help a couple patch up a marriage are as dangerous as amateur psychiatry. The most you can ethically do is to point out to the parents that a child's emotional health is endangered when he is left in uncertainty about what is going to happen to him. If you discover that plans have been made for the child, even if they are very sketchy, discuss them with him. Concrete and detailed provisions for his future care are more real to a child than general reassurances. If you can say something like, "You'll stay with your grandmother for two months and then come back and live with your mother and have your old room," you keep him from imagining himself deserted. If you can't talk with him about details like these, do what you can to convince him that he will be protected.

When there is a divorce, the children are commonly left with the mother or given into her custody by the court. In this case a boy suffers particularly, because he has no man after whom to model himself. Both boys and girls may feel insecure, because they are aware that fathers are the earners in their friends' families and they wonder how they are going to be supported. If you can impress the mother with the importance of letting the children's own father see them regularly and if you can talk with the father himself and convince him that he should make occasion to spend some time alone with each of his children each week, you may bring about great improvement in the children's outlook and behavior. When the father cannot be located (and when there is no stepfather to substitute), try to have a boy join an out-of-school club that has a man with a strong personality as leader. A teacher writes:

Herb's father and mother were divorced some years ago. Both remarried. The mother is expecting a new baby, and when Herb found this out his behavior became, if possible, even worse. Then his father was divorced from his second wife. Up until that time he had not seen Herb. Now he spends more time with him and Herb looks forward to their meetings eagerly. Herb's work has shown the greatest possible improvement. His main problem has been a desire to be loved by those around him. I do feel that, if his father continues his visits, Herb will show even greater improvement by the end of the year.

The birth of a half brother or half sister is another condition that seems especially upsetting to a child from a broken home. We discussed the bad effects of sibling rivalry in the last chapter. The child who is already uncertain of his parents' love is doubly doubtful when he finds that his position is to be challenged by a baby who "truly belongs." Doubly important, therefore, are all the measures that parents and stepparents can take to make the older child feel that he has a safe place in their affection and esteem. Older boys and girls in normal families can as a rule take the birth of a new sibling quite matter-of-factly. But a teen-ager who has lost one parent may be upset by jealousy of the baby and, because of the sexual implications, by jealousy of his stepparent.

The foster parents of an adopted child are quite likely to ask you for advice, especially if the child is a behavior problem in the home. When he is not a problem in school also, there is a possibility that he is being spoiled at home. If you give the parents sound advice about being firm and consistent, there is little chance that you will do any harm. At any rate, reassure them that he can behave well. Many foster parents, aware that their foster child is probably illegitimate, have a superstitious fear that "blood will out." If the child is physically healthy and mentally within the normal range (and if he has been adopted through a reputable agency he is probably both), do everything you can to convince the parents that behavior is learned, not inherited. If they are constantly afraid that they have adopted a doomed individual, the poor emotional tone of the home will produce the very results they fear.

When an adopted child misbehaves both at home and at school, his behavior may be the result of tenseness in the home or of the parents' failure to tell the child he is adopted though he has reason to suspect that he is not an "own" child. All authorities agree that an adopted child should be brought up with full knowledge that he is adopted. The child who knows from the beginning that he was specially chosen because his foster parents very much wanted him feels very secure. But if he suspects or discovers for himself that he is not an own child, he begins to imagine all sorts of dire things about his parents, both actual and foster, and about his future. The shock of discovery may in itself be very great. You must of course respect the wishes of parents who have failed to tell a child that he was adopted. But the situation is not usually one of your simply acquiescing in what you know to be the parents' wishes, however mistaken. Almost always friends and neighbors of the foster parents know that the child is adopted, and what they know their children know. Then the other children begin to tease the adopted child: "You haven't any mother," "They picked you up on the garbage dump." (We never cease to marvel at the vivid cruelty of children's phrases.) When this sort of teasing begins, no denial, however strong, will reassure the child. You must do what you can to call off the child's friends. If you can arrange for a skillful social worker who is experienced with adoption cases to talk with the parents, do. If not, ask them to read Adoption—and After, by Louise Raymond. In the meantime and all the time, you must do everything you can to build up the child's security and to give him the idea that you like him for his own sake.

Most of the cases of adoption with which we are familiar are ones where the foster parents love the child and feel proud of him. The children know they have been adopted and are proud

of their special status. They have no doubt that they are loved.
In contrast with this happy situation, one teacher writes:

Kate, age 12 years 10 months, Grade VII, was adopted as a baby but has
never been told. We've not talked about it, but I feel sure she knows, because
it's common knowledge in town. At times she is withdrawing and at other
times will do anything to attract attention. Her tales about home may be lies,
but they may have a kernel of truth. She told about how her "old man" had just
given her a new TV set and new bedroom furniture, and added, "It's about
time. I took a hammer to the old furniture the other night and really smashed
it up and got even with <u>him</u>." That day in school she was giggly and a complete
show-off. She never crossed the room without strutting and flouncing and was
constantly noisy. Another day, in art class, the first period, she quickly
sketched a very clever monogram, but while inking it in she made a slight
slip, became very irritated, said, "I like this," and then tore it up and threw
it into the wastepaper basket. The remainder of the day she was serious,
sulky, and nervous. Most of the day she was completely oblivious to her surroundings and her classmates and just sat and chewed her pencil or ruler or
bit her fingernails. At the close of school her best friend was waiting for her,
but she threw her head into the air and bustled past her without speaking.

PLACED-OUT CHILDREN

Courts and child-care agencies place many children in temporary foster homes, and correctional institutions often parole
youngsters to foster homes. In each case there is something
seriously wrong with the child's own home; either his own
parents are dead or unable to care for him or they are judged
not fit to have the responsibility of bringing up a child. Whatever the reason, these children have almost certainly suffered
severely from lack of affection and from insecurity. A large
number of them have never had the experience of living long in
one place or of feeling that any adult wanted them for themselves. Their own parents have dragged them from pillar to
post. The children have early developed bad behavior habits
that make them unwelcome in foster homes, and so they are
moved about again and again. Under such circumstances it is a
wonder that any of these children do adjust happily and grow up
to lead useful lives. But wonders do occur. One teacher, writing
of a very difficult boy who had been placed in a foster home by
an institution, says: "Several families in our district take in
foster children. I suppose when one family does it the others
discover that it is a way to earn extra money and do a lot of
good at the same time. Anyway, I have five other placed-out
children in my class, and none is the problem Irv is, thank
God! In fact, they are all natural, likable youngsters who get
along well with their classmates."
There are many reasons why foster-home care works so
well in changing children's attitudes and behavior. The shift

from the bad environment of their original homes is in itself a step toward a cure. A chafed spot will not heal if it is continually rubbed. A child who stays in a home where he is constantly afraid or constantly abused and where there is no saving grace of love cannot be expected to overcome these difficulties. The parents in a foster home, even though they take in children because they are paid a little something to do so, have been picked as people who like youngsters and get along well with them. If they were not this type, they could never put up with the problems that a succession of foster children pose. The foster couple are a couple; thus the child has the help and the example of both a father and a mother. The placing agency sees that the child is well fed and well clothed, kept clean, and given proper medical and dental care. A trained social worker is available to advise the foster parents and the child's teacher. The social worker keeps in touch with the school, and the parents know that they are obliged to cooperate with the school in every way. Of course, even with all these factors working in the child's favor, he may have been so deeply disturbed by his early experiences that he changes slowly if at all. But if you and the foster parents are patient, if you all work together to give the child the support of firm discipline but at the same time make it clear to him that he is wanted and safe and has as good a chance as anyone to succeed in the world, the victory will be won in almost every case. Here are two examples.

Jim, age 6, Grade I, was a state ward. He was illegitimate, and his parents had both deserted him when he was a baby. He'd been in five different foster homes and proved such a problem that he had always been "passed back" to the state. His present foster parents took him with their eyes open, because they wanted to have a companion for their only child, a spastic. My problem with Jim was to get him to understand that he did not have to fight, hit, and pull for everything he wanted. He caused more children tears than I care to recall. His new foster parents sympathized with my problem but said that they didn't blame him, that if we'd been pushed around like Jim we'd no doubt act the way he did. They were willing to work with me and to exchange news about problems, methods, and successes by telephone. Then I felt sure we could lick this problem. At home they treated the two boys exactly the same, and explained to Jim that he did not have to fight to get a toy. They kept telling him that they wanted him and that he was a member of their household. In school, I always asked him to return anything he had snatched or had hit another child to obtain. After a brief waiting period, Jim got from the child he'd hit the thing he'd been battling for. In the meantime, I went out of my way to compliment Jim every time he truly deserved it. Soon many children were saying nice things to him, too. After about three months, peace began to reign. Today Jim is one of my outstanding pupils. He's happy at school and at home.

Kit, age 15½, IQ 118, is a sophomore in high school. During the first month of the year he proved very difficult to get along with. He had no interests of any kind. He came to class looking like a tramp. He was constantly talking and disturbing the class. On occasion, he'd fly into a childish temper tantrum. His right arm was slightly deformed from polio. He sullenly rejected every advance that either teacher or students made. Investigation showed that he was illegitimate. His own father was unknown. His mother later married, but the stepfather refused to accept the responsibility for the child. The mother is now a confirmed alcoholic. Kit spent the first twelve years of his life in an institution. His mother did not see him in all these years. His handicap apparently prevented his being adopted. When he was 12½ his mother and stepfather agreed to take him. The next two and one-half years were years of misery and unhappiness. The family lived in a one-room apartment. Both the mother and stepfather worked. They spent their free time in bars. Kit began to threaten to kill them. The hatred he felt for them was extended to his classmates. The mother asked an agency to have him committed to an institution again. The agency, on investigation, decided that the boy should be placed in a foster home. His foster parents are ideal and experienced in the care of homeless children. They are overflowing with loving-kindness. The agency's social worker, the clinic of the Crippled Children's Society, the teachers in the school, and, not least, the students have all worked hard to help Kit. In the short time since he moved into his foster home he has changed completely. He gets along well with other boys and girls. His attitudes and interests in school are excellent and his marks satisfactory. Despite his arm, he takes part in sports and music. All this was accomplished by love and kindness and others' taking an interest.

POINTS TO REMEMBER

Insecurity and lack of love are the common lot of a child from a cracked or broken home. You may be the only person who will offer sympathy and pay attention to the child's needs and plans.

Scolding may make the child feel even less wanted and less secure.

Frequent friendly talks are perhaps the best means of convincing a child that someone is interested in him and will stand by him.

Praise from you for work well done and recognition from his classmates for group leadership bolster a child's security.

Plans for the child's future should be concrete and detailed to keep him from wondering what is going to happen to him. Try to show parents the importance of making such plans. Do what you can to reassure the child about the future.

A change of environment often works wonders in a child's attitudes and behavior.

Books and Pamphlets to Read

Adoption—and After, by Louise Raymond. Harper & Brothers, New York, 1955.

Children of Divorce, by J. Louise Despert, M. D. Doubleday & Company, Garden City, N. Y., 1953.

Room for One More, by Anna Perrott Rose [Wright]. Houghton Mifflin Company, Boston, n. d.

Your Child from 6 to 12. U. S. Government Printing Office, 1949.

Topics for Study and Research

Steps in the readjustment or progressive maladjustment of stepchildren, adopted children, placed-out children. There is great need of comparative long-range studies of such children to determine why some readjust well and become good citizens and others go from bad to worse.

School and Community Projects

A high-school course to prepare young people for marriage and family life.

"Family Courts" to handle marital disputes with a view to reconciliation when this is desirable and to skillfully planned provisions for the children in every case.

Family case workers employed by local agencies or the schools or both who will work with children from cracked and broken homes.

PTA Meeting

Films: Feeling of Hostility; Feeling of Rejection. McGraw-Hill Book Company, Text-Film Department, 330 West 42nd St., New York 36, N. Y. Roots of Happiness [the father's role in family life]. (Filmed in Puerto Rico.) Mental Health Film Board, 166 East 38th St., New York 16, N. Y.

Topics: The father's role in bringing up children. The content of a high-school homemaking course.

IX

Delinquents and Predelinquents

Len, age 13, IQ 118, Grade VIII, is rather short and heavy. He is usually neat and clean. He is a soft-spoken child, given to occasional outbursts. The other boys and girls in the class dislike him and try to get him into trouble with me. Even boys smaller than he is provoke him. He has a record of lying and cheating in school. He stole money from his mother and spent it on treats for the other children. When his thefts were discovered (by the police) and he could no longer treat, most of his "friends" turned from him. Len and another boy, possibly his only constant friend, tied up a younger child and left him on the floor of the garage at the child's home. The child would have been run over if his screams had not attracted a passer-by. Len's father was a wealthy banker. He's in prison for stealing the depositors' funds. Len's mother now works in an office. She's a heavy drinker and immoral. Len is interested in electricity and has made many ingenious gadgets. He wants to be an engineer. He is very cooperative with me and very responsive to the attention and warmth I show him. He does good work in class, the best of any of my students. But he is constantly tardy, despite promises of reform. He has promised me to join the Scouts, but hasn't. I very much fear that if Len doesn't have more guidance, more acceptance from his peers, and some improvement in his home situation, he will become definitely delinquent. The school psychologist reported, "He is filled with pent-up aggressions, fears, and uncertainties." These explode violently, as in the outbursts in my room and in his sadistic treatment of the neighbor's child. What can I do to help him?

—A teacher.

Mat was a student of mine when he got into trouble. He is now 22, but comes to see me occasionally. He was the eldest of six children in a poverty-stricken family. They moved from town to town and tenement to tenement. When he came into my eighth grade he was 13 years old, had an IQ of 118, was heavy for his age, and very handsome. We didn't have much in the way of a record of his past schooling, but he did good scholastic work for me. He liked reading, planes, and guns. But I soon found out that he was a member of the "Terriers," a gang of hoodlums from the slum in which he lived. He was frequently tardy and played truant regularly, but when he was in school responded well to my efforts to help him. He was put on probation for gang fighting. The probation officer told me that the father was an alcoholic, who had beaten Mat cruelly for every sort of minor and major offense since the boy was a baby. He was the leader of the gang. He was "girl crazy," and the gang's girls would do anything he asked them. After a week in which he didn't appear, the officer came in and told me that Mat had had his teeth knocked out in a gang fight and his face was badly scarred. He refused to come to school. While court proceedings were pending, Mat held up a store. He was caught and spent three years in the reformatory. He completed a trade course there and got a job as a mechanic when he graduated. When he was 19 he married one of his old gang girls, who was no better than she should be. They have two children. He's going straight now but is desperately unhappy.

—A teacher.

Letty, age 14, IQ 74, a student in a junior-high-school special class, was an illegitimate child. She's spent her life in a series of institutions and foster homes. Her behavior in school and in the homes has made everyone get rid of her as soon as they could. She's thin, nervous, excitable, and generally unattractive. This year she started to play truant. We found her in company with an older girl who was a known prostitute. Letty is now pregnant and is about to be sent to the home for wayward girls.

—A teacher.

Most juvenile delinquency could be prevented. We now have enough knowledge of the causes of delinquency to be sure that, if the personnel and facilities were available, the number of boys and girls who commit crimes before they are 18 could be greatly reduced, perhaps by as much as 75%. Moreover, we have had much of this knowledge for many years. W. I. Thomas pointed the way in his epoch-making book The Unadjusted Girl, published in 1923. William Healy and Augusta Bronner carried fundamental research still further, and published their results in New Light on Delinquency in 1936. Sheldon and Eleanor Glueck have brought law, anthropology, anatomy, psychology, and psychiatry to bear on the problem, and in Unraveling Juvenile Delinquency (The Commonwealth Fund and Harvard University Press), published in 1951, give a clear picture of the background of delinquents. Scores of other scholars and practical workers have explored both the causes of delinquency and methods of treating delinquents. Benjamin Fine has summarized professional opinions on delinquency in his book 1,000,000 Delinquents, which was published in 1955. Fine deals with the home, slums and gangs, physical and moral roots, the community, the schools, the police, the courts, and public and private training schools.

If society used the knowledge available in these books, there would be, instead of a rapid rise in delinquency rates, a sure though slow reduction. There is proof of this in the experience of the few communities that have adopted well-planned, even if incomplete, preventive programs. Why, then, is there so much talk and so little action?

Failure to adopt a comprehensive program of prevention is primarily due to the cost. This might be as much as six billion dollars a year. True, the eventual savings would be many times this—the FBI estimates that crime now costs us twenty billion a year—but marked savings would not be evident until fifteen or twenty years after the inauguration of the program. And, as every school administrator knows, taxpayers are loath to increase present taxes on the promise of future savings.

Moreover, the general public, ignorant of the fact that the history of the typical delinquent reveals frequent and severe corporal punishment, is convinced that all that is needed is a return to the woodshed type of discipline in home and school. Why spend money on psychiatrists when paddles are so cheap!

There is also a crucial problem in the shortage of personnel —of teachers, social workers, skilled policemen, and trained probation officers, of psychologists, psychiatrists, and marriage counselors. Even if the money to attract the right sort of people to these positions were available, it would take years to give them adequate training.

In the meantime, the school is the main line of defense. And, in any school program, the classroom teacher is the key.

THE SITUATION

There were 2,534,000 major crimes committed in the United States in 1956. A major crime is defined as murder, negligent manslaughter, rape, robbery, aggravated assault, burglary, larceny, or automobile theft. More than half the crimes against property were committed by boys under 18: 57.6% of the car thefts, 49% of the burglaries, and 43.6% of the larceny. Moreover, more than half of all adult criminals in the United States committed their first major crime when they were still under 18. In other words, if we don't prevent delinquency there are sure to be large numbers of juvenile delinquents who become hardened in their ways and grow up to make a career of crime.

Of 60,000 known narcotics in the United States in 1956, 7,800 were under 20, and most of these were criminally involved in the trade as "pushers."

Arrests of boys outnumber arrests of girls by 7 to 1. But in 1956 more than 150,000 illegitimate children were born, and 60,000 of these were born to girls in their teens. Furthermore, there is reason to believe that most prostitutes begin to ply their trade when they are teen-agers, or at least have their first illicit sexual experiences then.

These are depressing figures. They represent only part of the dark side of the picture. They do not include minor offenses or major offenses that went unpunished either because they were not discovered or because the police and courts did not press prosecution.

On the bright side is the fact that less than 5% of the youngsters of any given age ever get into trouble even in the big cities, and well under 1% in the rural districts. In considering the problem of delinquency we must always remember that more than 95% of our young people grow up sound, law-abiding citizens. We do not mean that they have not occasionally succumbed to experimentation and temptation or destroyed property—almost every man who thinks back over his youth will remember doing many things that might be classed as at least minor crimes, and not all women are guiltless. But only the unfortunate 1% to 5% persist in doing wrong, and it is persistence in wrongdoing that makes the true delinquent. The vast majority have been able to control themselves, and these include not only young people living among bad surroundings but also siblings of criminals. This indicates that we can, if we will, save most of the others.

THE CAUSES OF DELINQUENCY

If you have read the previous chapters, you will not be surprised that 75% of the delinquents come from less than 1% of the families. These are the families that have been broken by divorce, desertion, and death; where one or both parents are alcoholics; where the parents or stepparents dislike and reject and neglect their children; where the parents are mentally or physically ill; where the parents are themselves criminals or prostitutes. The experiences of young Mat, whose home was decribed at the beginning of this chapter, are typical of the young predelinquent and delinquent.

A great deal has been said lately about "delinquency crossing the tracks," and about the increasing number of delinquents from "good" homes. There is no doubt about the increase, but there is considerable doubt about whether the homes are good. The case histories we have and those cited by other investigators disclose that the delinquent from the middle-class or upper-class home has usually been in fact a neglected or badly brought-up child. His parents may have been divorced, or they may be living together in hate or indifference. The parents may be so concerned with their own ambitions— financial, social, or for prestige in their careers—that they have neglected their children. Social obligations have taken precedence over the children, who have been left to servants or baby sitters. (Many wealthy young men have had their first sexual experience with family servants.) The father has often been too busy with his own affairs to establish the warm human relationship with his son that is essential to the son's sound development. Very often there has been little or no supervision of the children. At night they have roamed the streets or driven their cars far from home. And discipline in the home may have been faulty: strict and even brutal, or lax, or inconsistent. The child may have been spoiled. The mother of a young murderer cried out in court: "Why did he do it? We gave him everything."

Some of the rise in the delinquency rate among children of middle-class and upper-class parents is probably an aftermath of war. Like their neighbors on the other side of the tracks, many well-to-do young married people started their families during World War II or the Korean War. War always causes hasty marriages and subsequently much disharmony and a high rate of divorce. Military duties keep the father away from the children. There are likely to be many moves, and moves intensify any feeling of insecurity that a child may have.

Of course, there are other causes of delinquency in addition to bad homes. A certain number of children commit crimes because they are mentally ill. Some boys and a few girls are misled by comic books, the movies, TV programs, and news-paper stories that feature sex and crime. These youngsters have naturally strong sexual and aggressive drives, and they find outlets in imitating what they see and read. A girl who pores over pictures of movie stars and beauty queens cannot help thinking that "lascivious carriage" is the way to fame, fortune, and a good time. Gangs play their part, but there is evidence that most members of gangs of delinquents were delinquent before joining. It is a case of "birds of a feather," except that to maintain his place in a gang a boy must always meet a dare, and so goes from bad to worse. Still, gangs are probably less influential in leading children astray than are older boys and girls who are already thieves or narcotic addicts or sexually experienced or perverts. Segregation of a minority group in a city slum stirs resentment and envy; the delinquent from such a district hopes to get revenge for the way his group is treated and to gain possessions like those of more fortunate families. Lack of wholesome recreation facil-ities may result in youngsters' being driven into unwholesome activities, though the evidence is that the incipient delinquent does not make use of recreation programs even when excellent ones are readily available. All of these causes play a part, but none of them operates in a vacuum. And usually they operate most viciously in homes stricken by discord or poverty, or both. In such homes, there is great danger that a child's emo-tional needs will go unsatisfied. In fact, W. I. Thomas' concept that every child needs love, security, recognition, and new ex-periences was first formulated when he was studying delin-quent girls. Girls, he said, became delinquent because, denied legitimate satisfaction of their needs, they sought in illegitimate ways what they felt they had to have. Obviously their parents had failed them.

PROGNOSIS

The Gluecks, with the help of a large staff of experts, spent more than ten years studying 1000 boys. Of these, 500 were delinquents—-persistent offenders in ways that in the case of an adult would result in arrest. The other 500 were nondelinquents. The two groups were very closely matched according to the neighborhoods in which they lived, intelligence quotients, racial backgrounds, and family incomes. The Gluecks found, as Healy and Bronner had, that the great majority of their delinquents had exhibited persistent, easily recognized delinquent behavior at relatively early ages. Specifically, the Gluecks found that one-half of them had shown persistent evidence of antisocial behavior before the age of 8, and nine-tenths before the age of 11. They stress that, while there is no unit cause of misbehavior—all the things we have mentioned may play a part—successful prevention depends upon discovering the potential delinquent as early as possible in his life. Since (if we omit hereditary factors) home conditions are the earliest influences to which a child is subject, determination of home conditions that are likely to contribute to delinquency would provide the best instrument for early prognosis. The Gluecks' comparison of their delinquents and nondelinquents revealed five areas where there were great differences in the way the two groups were treated. The following table lists the conditions that the Gluecks considered most significant and shows the percentage of the boys who were subject to each condition who were delinquent, and the percentage who were nondelinquent.

Home Condition	Boys Subject to Given Condition	
	%Delinquent	%Nondelinquent
Discipline of the boy by father		
Overstrict or erratic	72.5	27.5
Lax	59.8	40.2
Firm but kindly	9.3	90.7
Supervision of boy by mother		
Unsuitable	83.2	16.8
Fair	57.5	42.5
Suitable	9.9	90.1
Affection of father for boy		
Indifferent or hostile	75.9	24.1
Warm (including overprotective)	33.8	66.2
Affection of mother for boy		
Indifferent or hostile	86.2	13.8
Warm (including overprotective)	43.1	56.9
Cohesiveness of the family		
Unintegrated	96.9	3.1
Some elements of cohesiveness	61.3	38.7
Cohesive	20.6	79.4

The Gluecks state that, by discovering which categories apply in the case of a given boy and by adding the percentages assigned to each of these categories in the delinquent column, it is possible to obtain a prediction score. Only 5 of their delinquents had scores under 150, and 394 had scores of 250 or more. The Gluecks figure that when a boy has a score of more than 400, the chances are almost perfect that he will be a delinquent, but if he has a score of less than 150, the chances are less than three in one hundred. Several independent investigations bear out the Gluecks' claims. Other investigations, including a controlled experiment in the New York City schools, are in progress. In the New York experiment, two groups of boys, matched in scores on the Glueck scale and in other ways, are being followed for a period of years. One group is receiving specially full and intensified treatment, the other only the treatment usually available through school and community resources.

In forecasting delinquency, it is necessary not only to discover to which of the many possible <u>causes</u> of delinquency a child is subject, but also to determine from his behavior what <u>symptoms</u> indicate that the child is being affected. For, as we have said, when children are subject to the same conditions, some survive while others succumb. The Gluecks found that their delinquents' out-of-school behavior was often marked by a preference for risky, adventurous activities far from home, a dislike of organized recreation, e.g., in the Boys' Club, nonattendance at church, and extreme restlessness. The boys were often enuretic. The school history was marked by retardation, low marks, low achievement, and lack of educational and vocational planning. The relations with classmates were poor or only fair. School behavior was marked by inattention, restlessness, stubbornness, defiance, disobedience, laziness, lying, heterosexual and homosexual misconduct, stealing, obscene language, bullying and cruelty, destruction of school property, impudence, and above all truancy. (Our own materials emphasize the important place of truancy, obscene language, and physical attacks on teachers and principal as means of distinguishing the potential delinquent from the nondelinquent chronic offender. Of these, as Healy, the Gluecks, and others have pointed out, persistent truancy is the most significant.) Other signs that a child may be or become delinquent are extreme fads in dress and his possession of objects he would not normally have and so has probably stolen or acquired with stolen money. Some school behavior in itself constitutes delinquency: assault, arson, larceny, vandalism, sex misconduct, the distribution of pornographic pictures and literature, and selling liquor and narcotics.

TWENTY-SEVEN CASES

As an experiment, we asked twenty-seven experienced teachers from middle-sized New England cities, the members of a course in mental hygiene, to write case histories of delinquents whom they had taught or otherwise known in school. The widespread existence of delinquency is shown by the fact that all but one of these teachers had had contact in school with a delinquent, and all but three had had a delinquent in a recent class. Of the reports, 24 were on boys and 3 on girls. The IQ's were known in only 14 of the cases—and this is an indication of how little we are using knowledge that might help prevent delinquency. These IQ's were, in descending order, 120, 118, 115, 110, 100, 82, 82, 80, 80, 78, 74, 71, 69, 67. Note that more than a third were 100 or above. In the other cases the teachers estimated the pupil's intelligence all the way from superior to low-average. The reasons for these youngsters' being brought before a court were: 17, stealing or robbery (including 3, stealing of cars); 4, persistent truancy; 2, sex; 2, parental neglect; 1, assault; and 1, arson. The home conditions show a number of combinations of difficulties. The separate factors reported are: 8, home broken by desertion or divorce; 3, home broken by death; 5, both parents (including stepparents) working; 7, extreme poverty; 9, faulty discipline (including 6, brutal corporal punishment); 3, alcoholic father; 2, alcoholic mother; 2, criminal father; 2, immoral mother; 3, notorious fighting between parents; 2, feeble-minded mother; and 1, mentally ill mother.

The school behavior of these youngsters followed the pattern of the chronic offender, except that 6 were more inclined to be isolates than the nondelinquent child usually is. Persistent and increasing truancy was mentioned 12 times, profane and obscene language 6 times, kicking, hitting, biting a teacher or principal 3 times, and destruction of school property, frequently after "breaking and entering" when the school was closed, 6 times.

When as small a sample as this exhibits all the details forecast by large-scale research, we can be pretty sure that the principal factors are well established.

WHAT ABOUT PUNISHMENT?

The classic story of the futility of punishing one delinquent as a means of preventing others from following his example comes from 18th-century England. A child pickpocket was being hanged. A great turnout witnessed the execution. A record number of people in the crowd had their pockets picked.

The fact that punishment imposed on one offender does not deter others from committing the same crime is not an argument for leniency in the treatment of criminals of any age. Failure of the courts to punish delinquency promptly and consistently invites trouble just the way lax discipline in the home or school does. And scoldings and threats by judges are as futile as scoldings by parents and teachers. We feel that courts should probably commit more youngsters to institutions, not only because this keeps the delinquent and his friends from presuming on leniency, but also because the good institution often provides the best available specialists for the work of rehabilitating the delinquent and his parents. In the meantime, the delinquent is removed from bad home conditions and the public is protected against his attacks.

Many public-spirited officials and laymen, aware of the role of parental neglect in causing delinquency, are advocating that parents be punished for their children's crimes. This may, in fact it has been known to, have a salutary effect when a court inflicts a penalty on well-to-do and well-known parents who have let their youngsters run wild. If the parents are fond of each other and of their children, the shock may be sufficient to make them improve their supervision both in quantity and quality. And the court's action may awaken other parents in the neighborhood to the dangers their children face. But in the majority of cases such parents are not brought into court until too late. To inflict a fine on a parent who is already poverty-stricken, for example on a mother whose husband has deserted her and left her and her children to be supported by public relief or private charity, just doesn't make sense. Punishing parents who already hate each other and their children may destroy whatever hope there has been for improving the emotional atmosphere of the home.

WORK WITH THE FAMILY

A complete program of rehabilitation is the only way to help the majority of parents of delinquents be better parents, and so to rescue a child with delinquent tendencies and to prevent younger children from developing these tendencies. This requires intensive and prolonged social work of a high order. It means that the family must be given adequate financial support and adequate housing. It means that well-trained marriage counselors should help them straighten out their disagreements. In general, the parents will need financial support for many months and moral support perhaps for years. They may be willing to accept nothing but financial relief. They may permit a child to attend a clinic, but they themselves will not go to the clinic or admit a social worker to their home. In a large percentage of cases the best hope for the child lies in removal from his family, even if this means commitment to an institution. The exception is when a family has an adequate income and is essentially sound in its personal relationships, but has been endangering a child through ignorance. In earlier chapters we've described cases in which teachers have helped parents change faulty methods of discipline and rectify other mistakes in home care. Here is a case in which juvenile authorities, the family welfare society, and a school rescued the 7-year-old daughter of foreign-born parents:

Maria is 7 years old. She was born in Mexico, but her parents have been in the United States for many years. They run a small shop in the Spanish-speaking section of the town, and have never learned English. Maria spoke no English when she entered my first grade, but she is very bright and learned quickly. She was the only Spanish-speaking child in the room, and the others made much of her. In the afternoons, they'd take her home with them. Sometimes she would stay for supper. Her father would have a neighbor call the police, and when Maria was found they'd take her home, and he would beat her. When she came to school the second time covered with black and blue marks, I asked the principal to call the family welfare society. They investigated, and finally decided that Maria should be placed in a foster home until her father and mother could be brought to face and learn American customs of bringing up children. He and his wife proved as bright as Maria. The social workers spent a lot of time with them. Maria spent three months in a good foster home. The guidance counselor in the meantime worked hard with her. Now she's back with her own parents. They've bought a TV set, and Maria proudly invites her friends to come for the afternoon to watch TV and stay to supper. She has learned that she mustn't stay away from home unless she has permission, and that she must be home at the agreed-upon time. The separation seemed to me at the time a very drastic step, but it has certainly worked out well.

If the conflict between Maria's new American ways and her father's old-world attitude hadn't been resolved, there's no telling what might have happened. We've seen a number of boys and girls in roughly similar circumstances go to the bad.

THE TEACHER'S ROLE IN PREVENTION AND REHABILITATION

When no fundamental change can be effected in the home atmosphere and conditions, and when the courts do not deem it advisable to remove a child from his home or, if he has been released from an institution, to prevent his return home, the school must take up the burden.

Healy, in his comparison of nondelinquent and delinquent siblings, discovered that the deciding factor was often an adult outside the family who took an interest in the nondelinquent child. Most often this savior was a teacher who gave the child the love and recognition he was denied at home.

When the child likes his teacher, the orderly routine of school gives him an interlude of peace and security between the storms of emotion to which he is exposed at home. And the teacher becomes an ideal to the child, a person after whom he can model himself. The teacher's attainments, including, it must be admitted, the position of authority, set goals toward which he strives. The teacher becomes, in a phrase, the parent substitute who supports him while he learns to stand on his own feet.

The teacher who knows that he is dealing with a delinquent or potential delinquent and who understands the aggressive drives that are typical of these youngsters can do much to channel the youngster's energies into desirable activities. The Gluecks have shown, and extensive researches into the body types of delinquents and criminals confirm their finding, that delinquents are typically what is known as "mesomorphs." They are the broad-shouldered, sloping-torsoed, athletic type. Usually they enjoy good health. They have enormous physical energy. But they are inclined to dislike organized sports and athletics. They rebel against rules that they cannot escape. Given a choice, they avoid the occasions of conformity. The teacher of the young child may be able to show him that team competition and the rough and tumble of group play are fun. Older boys are more likely to take an interest in sports that emphasize individual courage and stamina. Boxing may be a means of teaching a boy to fight fair and obey rules and at the same time give him an outlet for his energy. One national boxing champion is an ex-delinquent.

The Glueck delinquents and nondelinquents were matched as to intelligence on the basis of the Wechsler-Bellevue Intelligence Test. This has two parts, one dealing with verbal abilities and one with performance on concrete tasks. Most of the delinquents did relatively much better on the performance side of the Wechsler-Bellevue.

In general, the abilities of delinquents tend to be practical. In school, they do better work when they are engaged in practical and mechanical tasks. Forcing predelinquents and delinquents with low verbal abilities to follow a curriculum heavily weighted with academic subjects frustrates them and increases their feelings of inferiority and resentment. At the elementary level they should be taught by methods that permit of a considerable amount of nonverbal activity. Later they do better in vocational trade courses than in academic high schools.

A teacher of any grade who is talking to a potential delinquent about his future may rouse his interest in training for a job that requires strength and entails movement. If a spice of adventure can be added, so much the better. The Gluecks state that many of their delinquents were hoping to join the armed forces. Certainly, many graduates of state schools for delinquents had superb war records. Our materials contain several thrilling stories of ex-delinquents who are serving the country well. One teacher tells of a high-school boy with an IQ of 120 who had been on probation for some time:

After the episode of stealing a car to run away, Neal decided to go in the service. He needed his father's signature, which his father, only too glad to wash his hands of the boy, gave gladly. The boy left school in the middle of junior year. The following July the FBI called on the guidance director and asked questions about Neal, who, it turned out, had been recommended by his commanding officer for work on a top-secret project. The guidance director was perfectly truthful about Neal's record with us and in court, and about the bad home background. The Army gave Neal the job. We don't know what it is, but he's going to marry a girl he used to go with in school. They seem very happy.

Another teacher writes:

Otto came into my seventh grade after he was released on probation from the state school. He was living in a foster home. I attempted to help him adjust socially without expecting too much academically. I felt Otto needed a great deal of affection, a feeling of being wanted. He did steal some things in our room, but I felt he was driven because he had nothing of his own. We managed to keep him on a fairly straight path for two years. I got him interested in water colors and in basketball, and he developed a great admiration for the captain of the baseball team. Otto became a pitcher, and our team won the championship. I was proud of what we had done for Otto, but we lost touch with him when he went to high school. He was arrested for stealing from his foster mother and recommitted. I didn't hear from him for several years until a few weeks ago. I was working at my desk after school and looked up to see the most handsome marine in the whole corps standing by my desk. It was Otto. He's been all over the world, and is now home on leave from his duty in Guantanamo, where he is a member of the military police.

A PROGRAM FOR PREVENTION

In any well-planned program for the prevention of delinquency, the school must hold a central position. The school is the first testing ground of the individual child's reaction to a social organization. Even in nursery school, a child is subject both to public opinion and to the control of a higher authority. The child who continues to rebel against his teacher, to defy rules, and to resist—and resent—the pressure to be a regu-

lar member of the group is antisocial. He is a potential delinquent, and may become technically delinquent by the time he is
7 or 8. But if the school early realizes how serious the implications are, it can do much to help the child learn that
friendly conformity with the requirements of a society is far
more rewarding than destructive opposition. When a youngster
has actually become delinquent, the school can frequently correct the causes of his trouble and guide him educationally and
vocationally in ways that will help him go straight.

The community must play its part, but few communities of
any size and very few, if any, larger cities have done enough
to stem the rising tide of delinquency. Community programs and
community committees that coordinate the efforts of the school
with the work of the police, the courts, the recreation agencies,
and the family welfare agencies are essential. In some middle-
sized and smaller communities they have cut the rate of true
delinquency and greatly reduced casual vandalism and teen-age
excesses. But, except for the recreation agencies, community
programs are generally aimed at correction rather than prevention. The delinquent is not known as a delinquent until he is
arrested, and by then it may be too late. The case histories of
the delinquents in one study show that they had almost all been
under the care of several social agencies. In some cases as
many as fifteen agencies had tried to rehabilitate a youngster,
obviously in vain. Agencies in general have neither the legal
authority to require cooperation nor the personnel necessary
to maintain the constant contact upon which rehabilitation depends. The courts, of course, have the authority. But Fine
reports that a case load of 500 delinquents for a single probation officer is not unknown.

The school has the legal authority to require the child's
attendance and, if it is willing to use it, to compel the parents' cooperation. More important, the school has, in the person of the classroom teacher, a professionally trained worker
of superior ability who meets the child day after day. Schools
are too crowded and have too few teachers, psychologists, and
social workers to do the thorough job of prevention that they
might. But even under present conditions, much can be done.
Each of the steps in the ideal program we outline below is
actually being followed by some school systems. It is not beyond
hope that the majority of the school systems in the United
States could take most of the steps in such a program. A single
teacher who gives thought to helping the maladjusted children
in his room may save many. If a whole school system made
organized, intense, and persistent efforts to prevent and combat
delinquency, the saving in dollars and cents would be very
great and the saving in human lives incalculable.

AN IDEAL SCHOOL PROGRAM

The preliminary psychological examination. Each pupil on his first entrance to school, whether this is in kindergarten or later as a transfer, is given an individual psychological examination by a qualified psychologist. The examination determines the child's IQ, forecasts his ability to do various types of schoolwork, and explores his personal adjustment. When there is any indication that the child faces unusual difficulties, either intellectual or emotional, the examining psychologist confers with the child's teacher and, if possible, with his parents. The preliminary examination is checked annually by various types of group test, and there is a periodic individual examination. Whenever the psychologist feels that the child or his parents need psychiatric advice, arrangements are made for this.

Home-school liaison. The school has at least the information about the home called for in our outline for a case history. When there is any indication of disharmony in the home, the home is studied to provide the information needed to apply the Glueck scale to the child. Teachers can be trained to do this, and any teacher who is alert to the importance of the father's and mother's attitudes and of the way the child is disciplined in the home will sense when the family needs skilled help. Every teacher visits the homes of the pupils in his class or home room and makes every effort to know well the parents of pupils who are chronic offenders. But when skilled work is needed, the family is referred to the school social worker or to a local family agency. Teachers who discover that a pupil is not receiving the parental love and care he should receive, go all out to make the pupil feel he is liked and wanted and to give him recognition.

Special grouping. Pupils with special handicaps are assigned to classes that are taught with the pupil's individual difficulties in mind. The special class for children who are considered potential delinquents is preventive rather than corrective. Early assignment to the class is important. (A large school or big city system can have a special class for the maladjusted pupils in first grade.) Assignment is made on the recommendation of the psychologist, who takes into account the results of his own examination, the child's score on the Glueck prediction scale, and the child's adjustment to the classroom. The class is small—ten to fifteen pupils. The teacher is a well-adjusted, wholesome person who understands and accepts a pupil's behavior as a symptom of maladjustment. The teacher has special training in mental hygiene, in work with maladjusted children,

and in work with families. But he is primarily a teacher and
not a therapist or a psychiatric social worker. He and the psychologist or psychiatrist cooperate closely. The psychologist
and psychiatrist are responsible for planning and interpreting
therapeutic measures like play therapy and group therapy. The
teacher, however, is trained to carry out the necessary steps.
The purpose of the class is to strengthen the child so that he
will be able to return to a regular class group and enjoy the
normal group activities and relationships. The curriculum,
however, is adjusted to the individual. The "performance-
mindedness" of the delinquent youngster is recognized and the
practical approach is emphasized. Because the strength that
a child derives from association with a friendly, understanding
adult grows with time, the special-class teacher keeps the same
group for several years. When a pupil is transferred from the
special class to a regular class, the special-class teacher
holds periodic conferences with him and may serve him as a
"big brother."

   The teacher as a big brother. The teacher who serves as a
big brother or sister to a predelinquent or delinquent pupil
maintains a warm personal relationship with the pupil as long
as the pupil is in school and, if possible, until the pupil has a
job and has shown that he can handle the job and himself. The
teacher is not a probation officer and still less a policeman.
He is, if necessary, the devil's advocate, the person on whom
the youngster can always count to stand up for him and help
him. The big brother must see a great deal of the youngster in
an informal way. This is a time-consuming process. Partly
for this reason, the big brother should not serve many
youngsters in this capacity. Moreover, the youngster should
not feel he has to share his big brother's attention with a lot of
other kids whom he knows as troublemakers. A regular high-
school teacher who can be released from part of his duties
makes an ideal big brother. The fact that he does teach in
high school appeals to the delinquent youngster's wish to be
grown up and gives him an educational goal.

   The system-wide committee on maladjusted pupils. The
committee is an esential part of the school program for com-
bating delinquency. The members include a school psychologist,
a school social worker, and a school physician when the community has the services of these officials. In smaller communities, the committee is usually made up of guidance counselors and principals of elementary and secondary schools.
There are advantages in including classroom teachers on committees when arrangements can be made to free them from
enough of their regular work to compensate for the time taken
by committee duties. The purpose of the committee is to

assure prompt, thorough, and <u>persistent</u> attention for every child who shows signs of becoming a behavior problem. The need for persistence cannot be overemphasized. The maladjusted child is very vulnerable to the stresses of change, whether this is in his environment or in the natural course of development. Many a delinquent adjusts well to one teacher and relapses with the next. And a great many become criminally delinquent in early adolescence. The committee, by seeing that each youngster is followed from grade to grade and from school to school, preserves the good accomplished by successive teachers and alerts each new teacher to the need for immediate action at the first sign of danger. The committee maintains a cumulative record. (A skillful secretary who is interested in the job and, though indirectly, in each child is a priceless asset.) Teachers are required to report, via their principals, every case of assault on the teacher, of stealing, of sex misconduct, and of truancy. The teacher may think it foolish to have to report the child who kicks and bites in the midst of a temper tantrum or the first-grader who out of natural curiosity lifts a girl's skirt. The good, experienced teacher feels quite rightly that he is able to handle matters like this himself and that it is foolish to make a fuss over them. The point is that the high-school student who draws a knife on the teacher is quite likely to have kicked his kindergarten teacher. The cumulative record of incidents that may indicate a tendency to delinquency discloses a dangerous pattern as it emerges. The teacher may be left to handle the first apparently casual misbehavior as he sees fit. When a series of incidents in the predelinquent pattern or an incident that seems serious in itself is reported, the committee goes into action. The case is given priority for psychological examination, for a home visit by the social worker, and for counseling by the guidance teacher. The proper community agency is asked to start work immediately. The policeman on the beat in the youngster's neighborhood, if he is the kind of officer who is good with youngsters and their families, may be asked to keep an eye on the youngster. Above all, each teacher, as he takes over responsibility for the boy or girl, is helped to understand the situation, what the youngster needs, and how the teacher can best supply those needs.

<u>Group therapy for parents</u>. The parents of maladjusted children benefit greatly from group therapy. A school system that has qualified psychologists or psychiatrists on its staff makes such work a regular part of their duties. Because the home environment is at the root of most delinquency, therapeutic work with parents is more efficacious in prevention and reform than direct work with the individual youngster, advisable as this is. When the school does not employ a qualified

group leader, it does all it can to secure one from the state or another outside agency. The school takes the lead in organizing the group and furnishes a meeting place.

POINTS TO REMEMBER

Delinquency can be prevented.

Better than 95% of American boys and girls are wholesome and law-abiding and grow up to be law-abiding citizens.

Early discovery of potential delinquency is a necessary part of prevention. Many predelinquents show symtoms of delinquency before they are 8, and most before they are 11.

A chronic offender who is frequently truant and uses obscene language is in danger of delinquency, especially if his home environment is bad.

As a teacher, you have an opportunity and an obligation to satisfy a child's emotional needs when these are not satisfied by his home.

Intense and persistent work is required to prevent the predelinquent from becoming delinquent. The curriculum must be adapted to the child's interests and abilities, generally with stress on practical subjects. He must be followed year by year and given extra support when he shifts from one school to another or when he shows signs of a relapse. A teacher who serves as a big brother to a potential delinquent year after year renders great service to the youngster and to society.

Books and Pamphlets to Read

Delinquents in the Making, by Sheldon and Eleanor Glueck. Harper & Brothers, New York, 1952.

New Light on Delinquency and Its Treatment, by William Healy and Augusta Bronner. Yale University Press, New Haven, 1936.

1,000,000 Delinquents, by Benjamin Fine. Signet Books, New York, 1957.

Schools Help Prevent Delinquency, Research Bulletin, Vol. XXXI, No. 3, October, 1953. National Education Association, Washington, 1953.

Topics for Study and Research

A longitudinal study of boys and girls who have been given scores on the Glueck scale, to see how accurately the scale predicts both delinquency and nondelinquency. Comparison of the results of such a study in schools in different types of communities with the results of the New York City Youth Board's controlled experiment.

A study of a pupil whose school behavior started in the delinquent pattern and changed for the better. Can specific measures, singly or combined, be credited with the change?

Anecdotal accounts of the work of a big brother with a delinquent or predelinquent, with emphasis on means of establishing rapport and maintaining contact.

School and Community Projects

Continuing committees on delinquency and maladjusted children.

Publicity that will show the relation of delinquency rates to neighborhood conditions. A study of the effect on delinquency when slums are replaced by modern housing projects that provide facilities for wholesome recreation.

PTA Meeting

Film: What About Juvenile Delinquency? Young America Films, 18 East 41st St., New York, N. Y.

Topic: Home, school, and community in the attack on delinquency.

X

The Unruly Teens

One of my teachers I liked particularly and always felt that we were on good terms. But one day for some reason I answered him back most disrespectfully. He quietly asked me to stay after class. He didn't scold me. He said he wanted me to state my opinions, but that if they were the kind I'd stated that morning, he wished I'd state them to him in private and not before the class. I thought about it that night, and next morning I handed him a note of apology and I apologized before the whole class. If he had embarrassed me before the class, or scolded me after class, I would have felt very resentful. He treated me as an adult and I responded in the same manner. I was a sophomore in high school.

—A teachers-college freshman.

I work in a high school where it is very easy to accept a group as a group, maintain law and order, teach the subject matter, and forget that the individual student has problems that are all-important to him. Why does Paul daydream as he does? Why is Quentin a defiant show-off?

—A high-school teacher.

I try very hard to make friends of my students and be one myself. Webster says a friend is "one attached to another by esteem, respect, and affection." I hope I can be that and a great deal more. I'd like to feel that any youngster with whom I'm in contact wouldn't hesitate to come to me with his troubles and ask for advice and guidance.

—A high-school teacher.

Because of the time element, it has seemed hopeless to study all the potential failures in my room. But the conference I had with one boy, a boy with an IQ of 140 who was failing day after day, has convinced me that I must do more. He told me about his mother's desertion, his father's drinking, and the fact that they'd been evicted from their home three times this year. He is now boarding with a nice family, but needs money to pay for it—his father can't. The dean has confirmed what Rick said, and she and I have gotten him a job. Even before then, in fact ever since he talked with me, he's had an A every day.

—A high-school teacher.

I am 65 but I take life with my effervescent teen-agers philosophically. They can't be changed, so they must be treated sympathetically and with understanding.

—A high-school teacher.

If you are a secondary-school teacher who likes his work, you probably think that the uproar over the modern teen-ager's bad behavior is the reaction of a lot of old fogies who have forgotten how they behaved when they were young. It may well be. Certainly there are large numbers of high-school and junior-high-school teachers who would not trade jobs with anyone. The vagaries of the adolescent are part and parcel of their interest in their work. And certainly the older generation has always looked askance at the younger. Two thousand or more years ago, a Greek wrote: "The young now love luxury, have bad manners, and contempt for authority. . . . They contradict their parents. . . and tyrannize over their teachers." The Roman poet Horace wrote that the young of his day were cowards and adulterers, not like the youngsters of his youth, "who tilled the soil with a hoe and chopped wood at the command of a strict mother." This tendency to belittle the younger generation as lacking in discipline transcends the boundaries of time or space. A current British editorial speaks of "spoiled children of a welfare state who have known no discipline." In view of this tendency, the results of a Politz Poll of American opinion are surprising and encouraging. True, 33.5% of the adults questioned say that teen-agers are worse today than they were twenty years ago, but 52.9% say there has not been much change, and 13.6% say that today's youth are actually better. Anyone who works with teen-age boys and girls to achieve a group goal, whether this is a sum of money to help refugee children or a higher average for the algebra class, cannot help being enthusiastic about the adolescents' generosity, willingness to work, and enthusiasm.

THE SITUATION

The rewards of teaching adolescents need to be stressed, because the difficulties, including discipline, are discouraging. We asked 454 seniors in the college course in six high schools to write essays on teaching as a career. Only 95 said they hoped to teach. Of the 359 who either had never wanted to teach or had changed their minds, 92 gave the problem of discipline—"the way students treat teachers"—as a reason. One student writes:

When I was in grammar school I thought that I would like to be a teacher. This desire followed me through my first two years in high school. But now I have lost the urge, though I like working with people. At the moment I think I'd like to go into social work. I might still want to be a teacher, but I'm not sure that I'd like to try to teach some of the little monsters (or mobsters) that now roam the high schools. I think I prefer social work.

The NEA survey of 4,270 teachers leaves no doubt that teachers in junior and senior high schools have much more trouble with discipline than do elementary-school teachers. More secondary-school teachers report that they have troublemakers in their classes, and they report higher percentages of troublemakers.

Our reports from students and teachers on actual incidents of misbehavior in secondary school draw a detailed picture of what students do that teachers disapprove and what the teachers do about it. The principal offenses (in descending order of frequency) are talking, cutting a class, failure to do schoolwork, rudeness to the teacher, tardiness, truancy, smoking, and cheating. Teachers report more failure to do schoolwork than do students. Girls report much more talking than do boys, and much less smoking. Neither teachers nor students report any considerable number of incidents of serious stealing, property damage, drinking, gambling, obscenity, sex offenses, or fighting.

In a study of 442 teachers with a total of 12,023 students in high schools in California, Herbert Zeitlin found that 52% of the boys and 30% of the girls were cited for disciplinary problems. Four-fifths of the problems fell into the categories of disturbance, disrespect, and disobedience. Cheating, theft, obscenity, profanity, gambling, and fighting accounted for less than 1% each.

CAUSES OF MISBEHAVIOR IN THE SECONDARY SCHOOL

The great burden of discipline in the secondary school is not, then, a matter of a depraved younger generation. Some of the trouble is due to two facts: that practically all youngsters now stay in school until they are 16 years old, and that the schools have neither the space nor the type of curriculum needed to serve a large proportion of these boys and girls. Crowded buildings and rooms provoke disorder. Large classes and the large number of students taught by each teacher make it hard for the teachers to know the students, to supervise them, and to guide them. A curriculum designed for the minority who expect to attend college frustrates the majority who are looking forward to taking full-time jobs as soon as the law allows. Many of these non-college-preparatory students suffer from the disabilities which we described in Chapter VI, "Scholastic Misfits." And all the other causes of misbehavior we have discussed—illness, physical handicaps, faulty home care, and cracked and broken homes—play their parts in causing disorder in the high school. But, by and large, most of the disorder among high-school students, both as individuals and as mobs, stems from the forces operating in adolescence.

THE AGE OF DECISION

If you are in charge of a sophomore home room, you may find it hard to realize that, by the time these young people of 15 or 16 are 19, most of them will be leading independent lives. From one-quarter to one-third of the girls (but less than one-tenth of the boys) will be married. Of the boys, 50% or more will be employed full time and most of these will be earning all of their living expenses. Many of the girls will also be employed. All of the able-bodied boys will be eligible for duty in the armed forces and a large number will be serving in the United States or overseas. From 30% to 50% of the boys and girls will be in college, responsible for getting themselves to class on time and for preparing their work, knowing that the alternative is flunking out.

The last three years of high school are veritably "the age of decision." Within those years a youngster must make up his mind about matters that will go far, perhaps beyond the point of no return, to determine the entire course of his life. In addition to decisions about education, employment, and matrimony, he faces problems like whether or not to smoke, to drink, to gamble. You may say that your sophomore is too young to do any of these things, but he sees slightly older teen-agers, as well as teachers and adults whom he admires, doing all of them. He knows that many of his contemporaries and adult acquaintances do not go to church and apparently have no firm religious belief. If he is religious himself, he begins to question whether or not he is right. If he has little religious conviction, he wonders if going to church is not a sign of hypocrisy— should he let it slide? Much of the fiction he reads hinges on sex. The newspapers and magazines he sees are full of erotic stories and pictures, many of them featuring teen-agers. He knows that many boys and some girls not so much older than he are sexually experienced. Is he being needlessly prudish? Why not give it a try?

Teen-agers, both boys and girls, are well advanced in their mental development. The girl of 16 or 17 is very close to physical maturity, if she has not already attained it. The boy is typically somewhat behind the girl in development, but he has more physical strength than he will have fifteen years later. Human nature provides for teen-agers' becoming independent and taking care of themselves. It has not yet adjusted to the slow pace of development, to the prolonged adolescence, which an industrial society makes possible and which modern civilization idealizes. The teen-ager is caught between two gigantic forces. On the one hand, he is driven by nature to assert his independence and to function as an adult. On the other hand, his parents and teachers and the conventions of our day tend to keep him, as the law says, in statu pupillari, a pupil. He is, remember, a child of our civilization. He shares our ideals and expectations. In fact, though he cannot but be aware of his developing powers, he is even more aware of how poorly qualified he is by experience and education to assume the full responsibilities of adulthood or to be accepted as an equal by adults.

The conflict in adolescence is thus not only external, not only between the teen-ager and his elders, but also internal, between the teen-ager's drive for independence and his fear of his own shortcomings. The conflict is between independence and insecurity, and the result is indecision. This indecision, coming as it does in the age of decision, produces the tenseness and anxiety that is typical of adolescence.

Unfortunately, both parents and teachers tend to treat a teenager in ways that increase his conflict. The parent is proud of his child's development and attainments and looks forward to the child's assumption of full responsibility. At the same time he fears the loss of love and companionship that will come when the child sets up a family of his own. Accordingly, he expects the child to show initiative and take responsibility, but he hedges him about with all kinds of restrictions, and may resent unduly any assertion of the right to make independent decisions. Parents can be deeply disturbed by the teen-ager's apparent preference for adults outside the family.

Teachers' attitudes toward teen-agers are quite likely to resemble those of parents. A teacher may expect a student to be responsible in every matter that is not covered by some specific regulation but never to violate or question a rule that has been promulgated. This attitude may be specially evident in the teaching of a subject. The teacher expects the pupil to learn, and to show energetic persistence in learning, exactly what the teacher thinks he should, without regard to the pupil's opinions of relative values or the pupil's own goals.

IN THE COURSE OF HUMAN EVENTS

If the necessity of dissolving the bands which have connected the teen-agers with their elders is not recognized by the latter, and if the process is not skillfully guided and assisted, there is sure to be a war for independence. Under the best of circumstances there will be misunderstandings and disagreements. Dr. George Gardiner, of the Judge Baker Foundation, in an article in <u>Mental Hygiene</u> for October, 1947, speaks of the teen-ager's "devaluation of parents," which "involves just those areas of action, those ideas, and those ideals which the parents have tried hardest to inculcate." The youngster who leaves his room in a mess, answers rudely, or dresses unconventionally is showing his parents that he is no longer bound by their restrictions. Gardiner points out that for parents to acquiesce in this behavior is to encourage a "pseudoacceleration or a pseudomaturity" that is not desirable. They must do what they can to exercise controls until the youngster is really mature enough to take over. The interval may be one of storm and stress, but, says Gardiner, parents can comfort themselves with the fact that 90% of the boys and girls survive the period without serious emotional upset. There is comfort, too, he says, in the knowledge that "it will pass—it will pass."

If you teach adolescents year after year, the knowledge that one class will outgrow its rebellious behavior is little comfort. You are confronted by another before you are in a position to join the first in looking back with pride and amusement. But you can take comfort and retain that degree of objectivity which lets you continue to enjoy your work, if you realize that much of the callousness, disrespect, disregard for regulations (including those governing attendance), and outright opposition to academic work is a symptom of growth. And it is helpful to know that you promote growth when you maintain standards.

The adolescent's need to establish himself as an adult in his own eyes and in the eyes of other adolescents makes him adopt the most obvious symbols of adult privileges. Adults drive automobiles. They smoke. They drink. The teen-ager who does these things proves, to himself at least, that he is adult.

The teen-age longing to own a car is so great that many succumb to the temptation to steal. Others sacrifice all of their out-of-school hours to earning money to buy a car. One football coach complains that his football team has been ruined because the boys who would be good players prefer to work for money for a car. That they are successful is evident. Most of the students in that school drive '56 and '57 models, while the principal drives a '49 model. He explains: "A new car means everything to them. To me, it would mean sacrificing a trip to Europe next summer—a trip I've been saving up for, for years." Luckily, the honest youngster can hardly manage to own and drive a car without his parents' knowledge and consent, and the school is thus relieved of much responsibility. Moreover, no moral stigma attaches to a young person's driving. Smoking and drinking present a more difficult problem.

A considerable number of our reports from boys in high

school say that they were "caught smoking and suspended." A few girls make similar reports. Occasionally the punishment is less severe, and sometimes a boy tells of an incident like the following: "I was sneaking a smoke in the boiler room. I came around from behind the boiler and there was my history teacher just lighting a cigarette. We looked at each other and he said, 'Don't get caught again.'" Many boys and girls say, "The teachers have a smoking room, why can't we?" In one case they petitioned the board of education for one. The public uproar left no doubt in the minds of students or officials that in that town the teachers were supposed to stop students' smoking.

Our reports from students and teachers rarely mention drinking in high school, and our materials from other sources suggest that teen-age drinking is more likely to be a problem at parties in private homes. Our cases occurred at graduation time. The boys involved were celebrating growing up by drinking beer, much the way their parents celebrate an anniversary by drinking champagne. The indulgence is not customary.

We shall come back later to the various measures the school can take to prevent students' smoking and drinking and to reduce the abuses of teen-age driving. The point here is that when adults, rightly or wrongly, prolong the restrictions against these activities or others that result from a desire for freedom and independence, the youngsters feel frustrated. This feeling of frustration in turn produces an aggressive reaction. The youngsters may arrogantly defy the restrictions by going to extremes. They may obey these restrictions but break others. But they may, if their parents and teachers have been skillful in their methods of discipline, control their behavior and use their aggressive energy in constructive efforts to prove themselves responsible.

Gardiner, in the article cited above, points out that the frustration-aggression cycle is typical of life from infancy onwards. The child early learns methods of handling his aggressive feelings, and the methods first learned may, if they are workable, last through life. They will be severely tested in adolescence and in every emotionally toned situation in later years.

INSECURITY

A 13-year-old panelist on the TV program "Talkaround" remarked: "Thirteen is an age when a child can make some decisions but not all. Both the teen-ager and his parents are experimenting in trying to find a balance between the youngster's right to independence and a continuing need for helpful adult guidance." Paul H. Landis says that "neither the adolescent nor his parent is sure how far it is safe for the adolescent to go undirected."

This uncertainty may drive a teen-ager into daydreams in which he achieves great fame without the risk of humiliation and failure, a risk that even minor efforts entail in actual life. Such daydreams, if they are not so excessive as to exclude the individual from normal activity and if they are not carried on into the later teens, serve a purpose. They let the youngster try himself out in imagination, and they may help him maintain his ideals until he is mature enough to withstand group pressure. On the other hand, uncertainty may force the youngster to risk both his safety and his reputation in the effort to prove to himself and his friends that he is not afraid.

When a teen-ager feels that he is on new ground or in danger of going too far, his security is greatly bolstered by having the company of other teen-agers. When teachers insist that girls should wear dresses to school, a group may appear in blue jeans when a single girl would not. Even where no question of pioneering or of defiance is involved, teen-agers find strength in the companionship of the group and in conformity with the customs of the group. While they cut themselves off from the support of their parents they seek support from each other. In union there is strength.

The teen-ager wants not only to be a member of a group but also to think he is a somebody in the group. He needs their recognition as well as their loyalty. He quickly discovers that he secures recognition by demonstrating his independence from adult control in ways that stir his friends' envy. There is always the chance that, in their striving for recognition from each other, teen-agers will begin to dare each other to ever more dangerous feats. They do not like to show they are afraid, and youngsters who are ordinarily law-abiding may suddenly find themselves damaging property or violating laws that they really approve. Sometimes they are shocked back into welcoming the control of adults.

When a New York theater announced a special "rock-n'-roll" program, youngsters, 5,000 strong, from all over the city began gathering in Times Square soon after dawn. They brought breakfasts with them so that they could stay in line until they were admitted to the 1,300-seat theater. A squadron of mounted police tried to keep the lines in order. The youngsters milled around and booed and threw their partially eaten sandwiches at the cops. The officers and their beautifully trained horses took the situation good-naturedly. Then the pressure of the mob broke a plate-glass window. No one was hurt, but immediate

calm descended on the crowd. Police reinforcements arrived
and were applauded. The youngsters obviously welcomed being
protected against themselves, and there was no more trouble.

YOUTHFUL FATIGUE AND EXUBERANCE

The youngster in his early teens is subject to enormous
swings in his available energy. It has been estimated that this
varies by as much as 40% within a few hours. Much behavior
that seems the result of laziness and uncooperativeness is in
reality a matter of fatigue. An Army study has shown that about
nine-tenths of the Army's trainees learn less efficiently than
they should simply because they are not getting enough sleep.
The youngster who says he doesn't feel like doing his homework
may really be tired out. When the pendulum swings the other
way, his excess energy and high spirits may erupt in a spontaneous practical joke or in an elaborately planned adventure.
For example, two boys teamed up to humiliate girls trying to
work the Coke machine. As a girl put her nickel into the coin
slot one boy would pull out the electrical plug. The other would
explain that a girl couldn't work even such a simple gadget.
He'd ask her for another nickel, slip it in, and, lo and behold,
the machine would work. In another case, two girls locked their
friends in the shower room while they hid all their clothes.
And, in yet another, a boy picked the music teacher's pocket,
secured the key to the band room, and gathered together an im-
promptu band—forgetting how much noise they'd make and that
investigation would show that they should all have been in study
hall. Tricks can cause an enormous amount of inconvenience,
as in the case of an anonymous telephone call to the police
that there is a bomb in the high school. They can also cause an
expensive amount of property damage, as when a hole was
bored in an assembly-hall ceiling so that a wooden "sword of
Damocles" could be strung up over an unpopular principal's
head. But, as long as youngsters have both energy and imagination, schools must cope with their exuberance—preferably by
making them responsible for righting the damage they do; for
example, by making up time lost through a bomb scare or by
paying for the refinishing of a damaged ceiling.

MASS DISORDERS

Mass disorder, whether it is a riot when the teacher is out
of the room, rhythmic shouting at an assembly, or destruction
of public and private property by an unruly mob of students on
the way home from a ball game, is the result of the forces we
have been describing. It is defiance of authority and thus proof

of independence. It enjoys the safety of numbers. It is exciting. It releases tension and gives vent to surplus energy. It is aggressive in the extreme and thus a means of working off frustration, immediate and accumulated.

Student riots are far more common in college than in high school. But great as is the criticism of college "panty raids" and "town-and-gown riots," the press and public are particularly harsh on high-school students who break loose.

Study of student riots shows that they are most likely to occur under four conditions: when there is extra tension, for example, that caused by examinations, graduation, or the approach of a crucial athletic contest; when there is an accumulation of physical energy caused by lack of exercise during bad weather or an examination period; when there is an acute feeling of frustration caused by the cancellation of some expected event, for example, when a game is washed out; and when there is a feeling of resentment, for example, toward a teacher or official who has imposed unexpected restrictions that the students think unfair. Under these conditions a crowd of students at a football rally or a graduation exercise or in detention hall can quickly turn into a mob. Some schools have bad traditions associated with hazing weeks or other special events. The prevention of mass disorder, like the prevention of individual disorder, requires that principal and teachers understand the causes of trouble so thoroughly that they will foresee dangerous situations and be on the alert to stop incipient disturbances. The teen-agers' drive for independence should be utilized by trusting them with increasing responsibility for making and carrying out plans. The relations of the individual teacher with his students are the controlling factor in both successful supervision and prevention.

GUIDE, PHILOSOPHER, AND FRIEND

The combination of the teen-ager's struggle to break away from his family's control and his feeling of insecurity as he assumes new responsibilities leads him to turn to an adult outside the family for guidance and support. If you are to fulfill this role, you must have all the qualities of a good teacher: friendliness, fairness, enthusiasm, vitality, a sense of humor, a liking for your work, and a liking for young people. The best high-school teachers relish the typical teen-ager's humor, exuberance, loudness, adventurousness, and cocksureness. They are quick to sense his sudden swings in mood, to respect his privacy when he withdraws into a daydream, and to succor him when he hints that he needs help. And the best teachers take a warm pride in watching their students grow in responsibility.

This is the great reward of teaching teen-agers. To achieve it, you must be really free from the need to dominate your students. You must encourage them to express their own opinions, though these may challenge those you hold most firmly and may contradict what you know to be facts. If you are young and uncertain of your ability to control your classes, or if, whatever your age, you suffer from arthritis of the mind, youthful challenges of opinion and fact may be hard to take. But only if you can let a student defend his own point of view will he learn to be open-minded enough to heed that of others.

You have to be extra careful to avoid the faults of your virtues. You wouldn't be a high-school teacher if you were not academic-minded and a good student yourself. You cannot teach a subject well unless you believe completely in its values. But you are at fault if you fail to understand your slow, practical-minded students who are intellectually unable to do the work that you think ought to be done in your class. You have to be skilled in the best methods of instruction so that you can adapt your classwork to a wide range of individual abilities. If you hide behind the age-old complaint that "they should have learned these things in elementary school," you fail in your duty to some of your students and you provoke their resentment. You are at fault if, in your enthusiasm for your subject, you fail to recognize that many of your students, including some of the brightest, have other interests that they consider more vital. If in your teaching you emphasize the techniques and information that are valuable mainly to the specialist, your students who hope to specialize in other fields will be bored. If, without regard to the rights and demands of other teachers, you pile on the homework, you overburden the conscientious student and stir the normal teen-ager to defiance.

You cannot make warm personal friends of one hundred and fifty or more students, but you can welcome those who seek you out, and you can seek out a few of those who seem to you in most need of a guide, philosopher, and friend. Try to arrange your time so that you can spare one or two of your "free" periods each week to listen to the youngsters who wish to talk with you. And try to set aside a regular time after school on one or two days of each week when you will be in your room and available to all comers. The nominal reason for meeting your youngsters out of class will probably be to help them with their work. You can make it clear that you want to help not only those who are falling behind but also those who have special questions or interests that cannot be taken up in class. But your real purpose should be to listen to those who wish to talk about themselves and their problems. Hosts of unruly teen-agers have talked themselves into a mature point of view while a sympathetic teacher listened encouragingly. As students learn that you are willing to listen, they will begin to drop in more and more frequently. They benefit almost as much if there is a small group gathered around your desk as they do when they talk with you individually. The group is in some cases actually more helpful, because one student may raise questions the others dare not raise and because all profit from an exchange of opinions. If they agree on a code of behavior, or on condemning certain types of misbehavior, they will abide by their conclusions and their example will influence other students. If, in the course of talking with a small group, you discover that one student has some special problem that would best be talked out in private, you can always arrange a separate meeting.

Perhaps the surest way of getting close to individuals and groups is to sponsor some extracurricular activity. Then you and the students share a goal. The teacher-student relationship changes to the more mature and more natural one of working together to achieve a common purpose. If you are a sponsor of an activity in which you think one of your troublemakers might take part, you can usually arrange for him to join in it. In this way you may be able to make friends with a youngster who would never seek you out voluntarily.

The teen-ager's devaluation of adults and consequent lapses from the standards and conventions that adults try hardest to inculcate obscure the mighty force for good or evil of adult example. The aberrations of the teen years are temporary. When the youngster is actually independent, he will revert to the patterns that he saw his parents and teachers follow. This is why people who have had happily married parents are most likely to be happily married themselves. This is why the most skillful teachers are generally found among those who were themselves well taught. And even while a youngster seems opposed to everything his elders do, he judges right and wrong by their ethics. If you set a good example in manners and morals, in dress and language, in work and play, the teen-ager who likes and respects you will think twice and probably refrain when he is tempted to do anything that is actually wrong. If in talking with you he has discovered that you share his secret ideals, he will have the strength to live up to these when they are challenged.

THE CORRECTION OF MISBEHAVIOR

Your liking for teen-agers and your understanding of why they behave as they do should not lead you to tolerate departure

from important standards. You can ignore or laugh at the girls
who seek attention by coming to school with their hair done in
braids and bows. If your community accepts blue jeans as
appropriate for school wear, you need not frown on them. But
when a girl begins to dress or carry herself in a lascivious
fashion, the school must put a stop to it. Permissiveness not
only interferes with the development of the self-control that
goes with true maturity but also deprives the experimenting
youngster of the support he needs. The teen-ager, like the
younger child, needs the security of knowing that he will not
be allowed to go too far. Only if he has this security will he have
the courage to venture and to learn by experience what he can
and cannot do.

Methods of correction must, however, take into account the
physical and mental maturity of the teen-ager and his emotional
sensitivity.

We've already expressed our belief that corporal punishment
does not produce good results and may produce very bad results, in addition to exposing the teacher to court action.
Certainly teen-age girls are beyond the age of paddling, and
teen-age boys bitterly resent it. If they are big enough and strong
enough to fight back, they feel that the chastiser is taking an
unfair advantage, if, indeed, they do not fight back and run the
risk of expulsion and arrest. The secondary-school student who
is not amenable to less-drastic forms of punishment will probably behave even worse after corporal punishment. In this
case it is surely better for the school and probably better for
the boy to expel him. If you do not agree with us, we urge that
you keep thorough records in all cases where corporal punishment is administered to see whether or not it improves the
individual's behavior in school and whether or not he becomes
a good citizen after he leaves school.

Our reports from teachers-college students show that, when
they were caught breaking regulations or otherwise misbehaving
during their high-school years, they expected to be punished and
took the punishment in good part. Most of them say that when
they become teachers they expect to treat similar incidents in
similar ways. But if they were to read all our reports, we
think they might see that teachers do some things that might
well be done differently.

High-school students differ markedly from elementary-school
students in their reactions to punishment. The elementary-
school child usually takes punishment as a warning and says,
"Well, I won't do that again." The secondary-school student
who admits he has done wrong is quite likely to take the punishment as a quid pro quo. He shrugs it off. Commenting on punish-

ments from scolding to paddling, high-school students make remarks like, "I felt nothing about it," "It didn't bother me at all," and, "I didn't think too much about it." Students criticize teachers who shame, scold, and nag. One girl writes: "After all, what could I expect of HER! When I become a teacher, if it ever comes to the point where I'm a nagger I'll quit and get married or something." Though students generally recognize the fairness of being deprived of a privilege they have abused and of being made to rectify damage they have caused, they accuse some teachers of being overhasty in the use of these punishments and of jumping to conclusions without giving the student the right to present his side of the case: "I would ask for an explanation and, if it was legitimate, let the student go with a friendly warning." And, feeling very grownup, students say some teachers are "childish" and "picayunish" about behavior that might better be ignored.

The increasing mental ability and maturity of secondary-school students dispose them to respond favorably to reason and discussion. Though many accept scoldings as a matter of course, all agree that the teacher who refrains from a public reprimand and talks with the student in private accomplishes much more. The private talk that shows a student why something he has done is wrong and why such behavior may adversely affect him in the future leads him to recognize that what he has done violates his own picture of himself as an adult. He is actually grateful for correction.

Several students approve class discussion of a fault as a hypothetical case. The individual student knows that he has committed the fault in question. He suspects that the teacher knows he is the guilty one. But his anonymity is scrupulously observed. He hears what his peers think of behavior like his and what the teacher thinks would happen to adults who behaved in similar ways, and he is left to make up his own mind why he should not repeat the mistake. Such class discussions seem to be extremely effective in isolated cases of cheating.

BUILDING RESPONSIBILITY

A high-school student writes: "The discipline in our school is fair. It could be improved a lot if we had a more active student council with adult advisors. I think a pupil will respond more to rules drawn up by fellow pupils than by adults who may not understand situations as they arise." But another student opposes his school's new student council because "as before, there's just a few kids who run it for us others."

In many classrooms and schools the students work with the teachers in maintaining order, planning to prevent disorder, establishing goals, and building morale. The visitor to a school like this immediately remarks the friendly atmosphere. For one thing, the students take it upon themselves to welcome him and see that he secures the information he wishes. There is none of that strange mixture of indifference and curiosity that an outsider meets in some high schools as he struggles to make his way through the noisy throng in the corridors. In the friendly school, the crowd is there and it is more often noisy than not, but the students respect each other's right of way as they make way for the visitor.

The good order which exists in schools where the students have made themselves responsible for maintaining it is not nearly as important as the experience in self-control and self-direction and in good citizenship that the exercise of responsibility provides. Teen-agers whose urge to independence is constantly thwarted by close, authoritarian supervision are bound to break out at the first opportunity. Instructors of college freshmen come to expect the graduates of certain ultrastrict preparatory schools to sow a disastrous crop of wild oats. Students from other schools, schools that grant freedom without license, can be counted on to adjust quickly and well to the still greater freedom they are allowed in college.

As we have pointed out earlier, merely setting up a student council does not guarantee that all students will obey school regulations. Nor do monitors and an honor system necessarily improve matters. Most students are much less willing to obey student monitors than teachers. An honor system is worthless unless every student in the school is determined not to cheat, as witness the scandal at West Point when it was discovered that many members of the varsity football squad were depending on cheating to maintain the scholastic standard required for participation in sports.

Here are some student opinions about student monitors:

I think the discipline in our school is atrocious. The first step in improvement, I think, though it doesn't seem a step in the right direction to many people, would be to abolish the hall monitors. After this, the decent individuals in the school perhaps could show that they are able to walk from class to class without assistance. Maybe the majority might catch on. I think a little responsibility given to the students, even if it only makes them go from door to door without a chaperon, would help discipline tremendously.

I am a monitor. One particular day when I was on duty, I had to ask someone to watch his step. There was a female history teacher coming up behind this boy. He turned around, passed a snappy remark, and swore. The teacher didn't do a thing. The very next day something very similar happened by one of the drinking fountains and the same teacher was present. I feel that if teachers, instead of playing the silent partner, would approach the student and do something about it there would be one of our smaller problems on the way to its solution.

Student courts to try offenders and determine punishments are said to work well in some high schools. They are, however, open to objection. The courts tend to inflict oversevere penalties on "us others" but to condone the offenses of a popular student who is setting a bad example. And there are frequent cases in which the principal has to reverse the court, either because it has been too severe or because the offense has been too flagrant and serious to be left to trial by the students. Once a court has released a "big shot" or been overruled by the principal, it loses all effectiveness.

If your students propose either monitors or courts, go along with them. But you should make it very clear that, as in the government of a state, agencies of the state will thrive only as long as they function fairly and efficiently. You must also help the students to see that self-government is a privilege to be earned and a responsibility that may be revoked.

We do not mean that a representative student council is undesirable. A council has proved useful in almost every secondary school that has one. The council serves as an advisory group to the faculty. It discloses points of friction. It suggests improvements and, when needed, changes in rules. It promotes and regulates student activities. For example, the council may determine the number of extracurricular activities in which a student may engage at one time. It may suggest the organization of a scholarship fund, arrange methods of raising money, decide how much of what is raised should be paid out in annual grants and how much invested, and decide upon the winners. When a council has a good tradition behind it, it attracts the most able members of the student body. They have high intelligence and they are in a far better position than the faculty to know and understand much that is happening or about to happen in the school. When the council and the teachers trust each other and are willing to consult each other, the decisions they reach are so reasonable that they command the respect of all the students.

Good student government grows out of grass roots in the home room. Home-room periods should provide time for full and free discussion of all matters that affect the welfare of the school. Home-room teachers should be skillful in promoting democratic procedures and encouraging the participation of each and every student. Responsibilities should be rotated so that each student gains experience in both leading and following. The teacher should be an active member of the group. Out of his experience he is able to raise topics for discussion which the students would not think of but which they will immediately recognize as matters that affect their right to independence.

They see that the discussions will help them to reasoned decisions about their future mode of life.

One bright senior writes: "There is never any trouble at football practice or majorette drill or glee-club rehearsals. The Comet staff always works well, too. In each of these cases the students are working with a teacher."

THE COMMUNITY PARENT—TEACHER—TEEN-AGER COUNCIL

Problems of dress, dating, hours for parties, driving automobiles, drinking, smoking, homework, and absence from school on special occasions are more within the sphere of parental control than of school control, but the school is inevitably involved. And when teen-agers take decisions into their own hands, the school is most often the place where they exhibit the results. Parents and public expect the school authorities to secure student conformance with conventions, even when the public generally ignores these same conventions and the parents are unable to make their children obey them. Cities, counties, and at least one state, Minnesota, have been meeting this situation by the formation of councils made up of parents, teachers, and teen-agers.

The simplest way to start a council is for the high-school principal to appoint a committee of representatives of each group. The committee studies what other communities have done, how successful they have been, and the methods they have set up for the choosing of council members. It is important that each community work hard to determine what method of setting up a council will make it most genuinely representative of the different age groups in that particular community. And the council, once elected, must be sure that the code of behavior it recommends is the result of sincere agreement on the part of all concerned. If it is not a true consensus, it will not work. If it is a consensus, it provides the parents with a set of standards that they can insist upon without any argument about the truth of the statement that "all the other kids do." More important, an approved code provides the youngsters themselves with a set of standards that help them refrain from going too far under pressure from friends. They can refuse a dare to drink and not feel cowardly.

A model code, which parents, teachers, and teen-agers in Minnesota have worked out together, shows that teen-agers readily agree with wise restrictions. The suggested code says that dress should suit the occasion, that youngsters should return directly home from parties unless other plans have been approved by parents, that junior-high students should not "go steady," that riders share with drivers the responsibility for safe driving, that youngsters should understand it is proper to decline an alcoholic drink, that there should be no gatherings for junior-high students on school nights, and that senior-high gatherings should be over by ten o'clock on school nights.

Every account of community councils we have seen features the youngsters' conservatism in matters of drinking. The great majority of teen-agers are emphatic that alcoholic beverages should not be served at their parties. There is usually wider difference of opinion about smoking and about matters of dress and hours. But the gap is never hopeless, and when consensus is reached, the school has a sure answer to its critics, young and old.

NEW COURSES

Thirty years ago, farsighted administrators were discussing "the new fifty per cent" among high-school students. They saw that the time was at hand when all teen-agers would attend high school instead of the old fifty per cent who went to high school as a means of preparing themselves for college. The full enrollment has come, but high schools are still failing to meet the needs of the new type of student. In 1956, a New York State Education Department survey of a suburban county with a population of more than 1,000,000 revealed that 75% of the boys and girls attending high schools in the county had no opportunity to take a technical or trade course. If these youngsters stay in school they will have to take a college-preparatory course, though only 40% of the students in the county schools expect to go to college.

The failure of most high schools to serve the needs of large percentages of their students is the main cause for the number of students who drop out of school before they graduate. If they just dropped out as soon as they and their teachers felt that the school had nothing to offer them, and if they were able to obtain suitable employment, little if any harm would be done. As it is, they linger in school until they are old enough to obtain working papers, or even longer. In the meantime they become serious behavior problems. They are a drain on their teachers' time and energies. They interfere with students who want to learn. And they acquire a taste for idleness and disorder that may become habitual.

Many high-school principals and teachers have worked hard to meet the needs of the new fifty per cent. That more has not been accomplished is due to the typical school board's fear of extra expense and to the conservatism and inertia of the public.

Even when a school offers good non-college-preparatory courses that a student wishes to take, his parents may be unwilling to accept a counselor's advice that he give up the college course. In their minds, the old-style high-school education is a social advantage they want for their children.

Despite public and official opposition and lack of funds, there have been some notable advances. The most common are an expansion of vocational courses in both trade schools and high schools. These courses prepare qualified students for the skilled trades and less able students for the semiskilled trades. The business curriculum has been redesigned so as to prepare not only girls for secretarial and office work but both girls and boys for positions in retail trade.

Actual work experience is both appealing and valuable to the new fifty per cent. Paid in-school employment on the model of the very successful Youth Administration Program of the 'thirties is being revived. There are several good part-time apprentice-training programs run in cooperation with local industries on the model of trade-school apprentice programs and England's continuation schools. Newark, New Jersey, is conducting an interesting experiment in a summer work program which employs students on the city's watersheds in the long vacation. Unpaid work experience is gained in the community service program sponsored by the Millbrook (New York) School and depicted in the film Beyond the Schoolroom. (This is obtainable from the Columbia University Press.)

Courses in leisure-time activities and extensive but practical courses in health education are good preparation for adult life. The usual allotment of two hours a week to physical education is absurdly small. More time devoted to learning sports and playing them would build youngsters' bodies and give them a knowledge they would use in later life as players and as spectators. After all, we live in a civilization where professional ball players receive a minimum salary higher than the maximum for teachers. More time in health education would improve the health of the students themselves and prepare them better to care for their children.

Instruction of high-school students in the effects of drugs and alcohol is required by law in most states, but too often the observance of the law is merely perfunctory. In an article, "An Elective for Teachers: Narcotics and Other Drugs" (Teacher Education Quarterly, Connecticut State Board of Education, Vol. XII, No. 3, Spring, 1955), William C. Forbes outlines a course that might be adapted for use in secondary schools. The course covers the chemistry and physiological effects of drugs in general and a review of human physiology. Nicotine, caffeine, and aspirin are discussed, as well as alcohol and narcotics. Forbes shows how taking up the chemistry and physiological effects of common drugs like aspirin and nicotine makes possible a matter-of-fact approach to alcohol and narcotics. The student who learns facts in a common-sense way is not inclined to experiment with dangerous drugs just for a thrill or to abuse the socially accepted drugs. Similar instruction is offered in Grades VII-XII in Vancouver, British Columbia, as a part of the normal health and development course.

Courses in human relations and psychology have an important place in the new high-school curriculum. They serve the needs both of the new fifty per cent and of those who expect to go to college. The usual homemaking course is a step in the right direction, but it does not go far enough. Teen-agers are intensely interested in improving their relations with their contemporaries and eagerly extend their search for knowledge to all aspects of family living. Sex education is a necessity. So also is education in courtship and in married life. If our high schools gave good courses along these lines, the vicious circle of unhappy marriages that produce maladjusted children who in turn contract unhappy marriages might be broken.

Driver-training courses are perhaps the most widely offered of all the possible additions to the old-style curriculum. They have done much to improve the skills of teen-age drivers and to give them respect for safety. The problems that the other courses we have suggested are designed to meet are in their ways as grave as the problem of automobile safety. Perhaps the public will soon realize that all high-school programs should be designed to train students to live better.

ADMINISTRATION AND ORGANIZATION

Ability grouping is still frowned upon by a few school administrators, and, in high schools that employ it, not a few teachers fail to take advantage of the opportunities it gives to adapt materials and methods to the abilities and interests of individual students. The result is a large crop of acute disciplinary difficulties followed by a large percentage of drop-outs.

Our reports show that in many schools disorderly pupils are referred to the guidance counselor rather than to the principal. Counselors generally object to this unless they can take the time to counsel. But their objections are often overruled, and in too many instances, according to our reports, all the counselor does is to scold the student or give him a pep talk. Administrators should try to arrange a guidance setup under which a disorderly pupil is carefully studied in an attempt to find out why he is disorderly and to determine his abilities and discover his interests. A youngster who can be guided to adopt a realistic goal and to see how his school program will help him achieve it is a sure candidate for reform.

High-school students frequently complain that some of their teachers are so out of tune with adolescents that they are bound to have disciplinary trouble. One girl writes: "I don't want to be a teacher. I am not old and gray enough." A boy says: "During the past four years we have been subjected to a wide variety of teachers: fat, small, tall, funny, stimulating, and sometimes dull." The administrator should be aware that, valuable as knowledge of a subject and enthusiasm for it are, knowledge of youngsters is even more important. The high-school teacher is still an integral part of the college-preparatory tradition. He has shown a strange reluctance to adapt his teaching and his methods to the noncollege type of student, even when such students make up the majority of his classes. He does not realize that the proper study of the teacher is the student. Administrators have the obligation to arrange in-service training for their staffs, training of a caliber that will convince the most academic-minded of teachers that there are sciences of education and psychology and that these can be both interesting and practical. There is a great deal of truth in the remark of one senior: "Psychology, in my estimation, is more important to a teacher's background than anything else. I think the lack of this in high-school teachers has caused the students' feeling of disrespect toward the teachers."

When high schools were smaller and more nearly homogeneous, a close relationship existed between students and teachers. In those days there was most often but one teacher for each subject. He taught the same students for four years and got to know them very well. The day of the small, intimate school is past forever. There is little prospect of any marked reduction in the number of pupils that each high-school teacher must instruct each year. On the contrary, rising enrollments and a diminishing supply of teachers may force the substitution of TV lectures for personal contact. Shifting the emphasis from teaching to learning may not be altogether bad. But it will sacrifice much that is fine and enjoyable and rewarding in our profession. As a partial counter, schools should be organized so that the same teacher retains the same group of students in his home room and, so far as possible, in his classes throughout their years in high school. Three or four years of association would mean that students and teachers could learn to know each other well and would give the student a guide on whom he could depend until he achieved independence.

POINTS TO REMEMBER

Teen-agers are not as bad as their elders are wont to think. If you like them, they will like and respect you.

The drive for independence is nature's way of preparing the teen-ager for the independence he must so soon assume.

The teens are the age of decision. Teen-agers need experience in making responsible decisions, but they need guidance, too.

While the teen-ager is breaking away from his parents, he tends to seek the support of another adult. If he turns to you, the standards you insist upon and the example you set may determine the pattern he will follow in later life.

Reasoning is more potent than punishment in correcting teenage misbehavior. The appeal of reason is the appeal of maturity.

Prevention of disorder requires that you understand its causes and be alert in exercising control. More important, you must channel the teen-ager's drive for independence into activities which he is responsible for planning and carrying out.

Student participation in school government is most effective when it springs from the belief of all students that certain rules are necessary and certain forms of behavior undesirable. When the students are convinced that something should or should not be done, they welcome faculty support in attaining their goals.

Teen-agers, despite all their tendencies to flock, are individuals. You must plan to accommodate both what you teach and the way you teach it to the individual's interests and abilities.

Books and Pamphlets to Read

Adolescence and Youth — The Process of Maturing, by Paul H. Landis. Second edition, McGraw-Hill Book Company, New York, 1952.

High School Discipline in American Society, The Bulletin of the National Association of Secondary-School Principals, Vol. 40, No. 216, January, 1956.

Youth — The Years from Ten to Sixteen, by Arnold Gesell, Frances L. Ilg, and Louise B. Ames. Harper & Brothers, New York, 1956.

Topics for Study and Research

The academic potential of high-school students with dull-normal and low-average intelligence.

The newspaper and magazine reading of adolescents and its effect on their attitudes and behavior.

A comparison of the behavior records and backgrounds of drop-outs with those of graduates matched as to intelligence. Is a pattern evident that would serve as a basis for prognosis?

School and Community Projects

A truly representative student government.

A parent—teacher—teen-ager community council.

A curriculum designed to meet the needs of the students who expect to enter factories or the service trades as soon as they legally can.

PTA Meeting

Films: Adolescent Development (five films: The Meaning of Adolescence, Physical Aspects of Puberty, The Age of Turmoil, Social-Sex Attitudes in Adolescence, and Meeting the Needs of Adolescents). McGraw Hill Book Company, Text-Film Department, 330 West 42nd St., New York 36, N. Y.

Topic: The unruly teens.

XI

Discipline for Maturity:
The Teacher's Role in Mental Hygiene

Seth, age 7, Grade II, is the youngest of three children. The oldest, a girl, died a few years ago, the middle, a boy, is in the "Children's Institute," and Seth at home with his parents. The conditions at home are very poor. Both parents work, and Seth often finds no one home after school. There's talk of a divorce. The father drinks. He beats the mother in Seth's presence. In school Seth is friendly as long as he can dominate. When he cannot, he sulks and attacks others. Until a month ago I thought I was making progress with Seth. Then a new pupil came in the room, of whom I made much to help him "settle in." Seth now tries to provoke and irritate me one day and is nice the next. I cannot see what brings on the sulks. I fear he feels rejected in school as at home. P.S. After writing this I heard Seth in passing whisper to another child, "I love Miss Dove." Looks like we're a couple still in love but just don't get along any more.

—A teacher.

Ted, age 9, Grade IV, IQ 119, is the son of an engineer who travels a great deal. He's what I call a "cloud rider." But when he's not daydreaming, he is very aggressive. He steals something practically every day—anything, from paper clips to money—but drops what he's taken on the playground where it can be found. I went to see his mother. She seems flighty and unconcerned. His father took Ted to a psychiatrist, who, according to the mother, said all Ted needed was loads of love and attention.

—A teacher.

Upton, age 13, Grade VIII, was transferred to our elementary school from the junior high school on the recommendation of the psychiatrist. The doctor thinks he should be in a school for emotionally disturbed children, but the parents, though not poor, cannot afford the fee. The clinic says he is "highly disturbed" and "given to infantile behavior." It was thought our setup would be less disturbing than the junior high. Upton has violent temper outbursts directed against his mother or me or other children or himself—whoever he thinks is responsible for any difficulty. I told the other pupils about Upton, and they are very patient with him and have elected him to office. His control has improved. But I don't know how much or how little to ask of him. He's very bright, but a request, no matter how gentle, may bring an outburst.

—A teacher.

Mental illness and personal maladjustment are paramount human problems, and you as a teacher have a vital role in their solution. Earlier chapters have dealt with the common causes of maladjustment as it is evident in disorderly behavior in the classroom. Here we are concerned with the pitiful fate of the disorderly pupil if he does not find help in overcoming his difficulties.

DEFINITIONS

Mental illness may be defined as impairment of the mind to a degree that interferes with the individual's ability to manage his own affairs and to perform his duties in a manner acceptable to society. Mental illness takes various forms, some more serious than others. The person who suffers from unwarranted anxiety, depression, false fears, and psychosomatic illnesses is not mentally well, though he may be able to hold a job and live with his family. Anxiety or depression or any emotional state may be exaggerated to the point where it excludes normal human activities. Schizophrenia (characterized by hallucinations, the so-called "split personality") and paranoia (characterized by delusions of persecution) are two common types of mental illness. Schizophrenia tends to appear early in life. Some psychiatrists think that there is no essential difference between schizophrenia and paranoia, or indeed between any forms of mental illness. The practical problem is to judge when a person is so seriously affected that his welfare and the welfare of the public require his hospitalization.

Maladjustment is a term that is rather loosely used. It implies inability to adapt oneself to the circumstances of one's life. Dr. Ian Skottowe (Clinical Psychiatry, McGraw-Hill Book Company, New York, 1954) speaks of the maladjusted child as one who, though he has no formal mental illness, "has some difficulty of social or interpersonal adaptation" evident in behavior problems (such as truancy, lying), disturbances of personality (such as excessive shyness or aggressiveness), habit disorders (such as nail biting, tics), and nocturnal disturbances (such as enuresis). Adults who are criminals, perverts, unhappily married, or unhappily employed might be called maladjusted.

Mental health, according to the National Association for Mental Health,

is far more than merely the absence of mental illness. Mental health is something all of us want for ourselves, whether we know it by name or not. When we speak of happiness, or peace of mind, or enjoyment, or satisfaction, we are usually thinking about mental health. Mental health has to do with everybody's daily life. It means the over-all way that people get along—in their families, at school, on the job, at play, with their associates, in their communities. It has to do with the way each person harmonizes his desires, ambition, ideals, feelings and his conscience in order to meet the demands of life as he has to face it. It has to do with: (1) how you feel about yourself; (2) how you feel

about other people; (3) how you are able to meet the demands of life. There is
no line that neatly divides the mentally healthy from the unhealthy. There are
many different degrees of mental health. No one characteristic by itself can
be taken as evidence of good mental health, nor the lack of any one as evidence
of mental illness. And nobody has all the traits of good mental health all of
the time.

We may define mental health concisely as the ability to adjust
satisfactorily to the various strains we meet in life. and mental
hygiene as the means we take to assure this adjustment.

THE CAUSES OF MENTAL ILLNESS

Though everyone is liable to mental illness or to some degree of maladjustment. some people are able to resist conditions that overcome others. One theory is that susceptibility is
a matter of blood chemistry. Certainly a constitutional factor
cannot be ruled out. But equally certain is the fact that resistance can be increased by the practice of good mental hygiene.
The first step in this is to understand as much as possible
about the conditions that contribute to maladjustment. Briefly.
these are physical defects (resulting from disease. injury. especially brain injury, and malnutrition) and sudden, severe.
or prolonged emotional and psychological strains. (See Ian
Skottowe. op. cit.)

There is general agreement that the early years of the
child's life are of the utmost importance. for good or ill. in
mental health. The same influences that tend to cause chronic
misbehavior in a child are those that contribute to mental illness and maladjustment—indeed. chronic misbehavior is a
form of maladjustment. A child who lacks parental love and
care and feels insecure about his home is particularly vulnerable. And he is most particularly vulnerable if he lacks love
when he is very young and if he continues to suffer from insecurity for a period of years. If he is not wisely handled when he
reaches school. if he is constantly scolded or punished. if he is
asked to do work beyond his capacity, if he is excluded from the
activities of the other children, his feelings of being unloved
and of insecurity are increased and prolonged. The school.
which can be an instrument of rescue. may instead damage a
child severely.

STATISTICS ON MENTAL ILLNESS

Perhaps you will never have a pupil in class who is as seriously disturbed as Upton, whose case is cited at the head of this
chapter. But if maladjustment and mental illness continue to develop at the present rate. an average of three out of any class

of thirty pupils will become seriously maladjusted in later life, and one or more of these will have to be hospitalized for mental illness.

At present, half of all the hospital beds in the United States are occupied by patients who are mentally ill. There are three-quarters of a million of these patients—more than the combined total of those suffering from polio, cancer, heart disease, and tuberculosis. Of the 750,000, 375,000 suffer from schizophrenia. In addition to those who are confined to hospitals, there were, in 1956, 2,500,000 men, women, and children who were being treated in clinics, psychiatrists' offices, or as hospital out-patients for some form of mental illness. It is estimated that, all told, at least 10,000,000 Americans, 1 in 16 of us, are now suffering from some form of mental disorder, and that 10% of the children in our schools are emotionally disturbed to the point where they need professional help.

Grave as the situation is, there are gleams of hope. About 45% of the patients admitted to state hospitals for the mentally ill are discharged as cured or improved. In some institutions, from 65% to 80% of the first admissions are discharged within a year. Of those suffering from schizophrenia, which used to be thought incurable, 55% to 60% now recover or improve. Though 1956 was a record year for first admissions to mental hospitals, the number of mental patients who were hospitalized at the end of the year was 7,000 below the number for the previous year. This is the first decline in number since nationwide statistics have been kept. Our knowledge of care and treatment has advanced on a broad front, and research with new drugs promises great gains.

One development of special interest to teachers is the increase in the number of hospitals designed and staffed for the care and treatment of emotionally disturbed children. Pioneer work has been done in the Children's Psychiatric Unit at the University of Michigan Hospital, and many states now have or soon will have similar units.

THE TEACHER'S ROLE IN MENTAL HYGIENE

As a teacher you have a double role to play in the mental hygiene of your pupils. You can identify children who are subjected to adverse influences and institute measures to correct these before they are so prolonged as to overstrain the child. And you can build good mental health in your pupils so that they will be better able to withstand or recover from the inevitable strains of life. Because you associate with the child day after day, you know when he is in danger and can work constructively with him. Moreover, because of your training in child psychology and child development, you have the technical knowledge to help him or, when necessary, to secure other help for him.

THE SYMPTOMS OF MALADJUSTMENT

You may not find it easy to decide when a pupil's behavior is a symptom of maladjustment. Most children will at one time or another fail to meet some of the demands of life in the classroom. They will be overaggressive and overactive, or they will withdraw from the activities of the other boys and girls. Occasional "abnormal" behavior may be due to some temporary strain or it may actually represent an attempt at learning how to adjust to a situation, for example, by angry retaliation to teasing.

Four criteria are useful in judging the seriousness of a child's behavior. Is the behavior unusual for one of his age? Does it occur with unusual frequency? Is it unusual in its intensity? Is it unusual in its duration? Take temper as an example. Many kindergarten children will have temper tantrums, and at this age tantrums are not necessarily a bad sign unless they occur with unusual frequency, reach unusual intensity, and last unusually long. A 7-year-old may have an occasional tantrum, but by that age frequent tantrums are not to be expected. In a high-school youngster, a real tantrum is definitely unusual.

The misbehavior of the typical chronic offender often constitutes a symptom of maladjustment according to all four of the criteria of unusualness. It may be relatively immature, and it may be frequent and intense and continue for years.

Maladjustment may show itself in unusually frequent, severe, or prolonged fears, worry, forgetfulness, timidity, daydreaming, imaginative lying, stealing, trembling, twitching, blinking, insomnia, oversleeping, lethargy, jealousy, cruelty, aggressiveness, physical activity, and truancy. To these should be added any continuing physical disturbance for which there is no physical cause; for example, obesity, failure to gain weight, vomiting, enuresis, fatigue, headaches, and bad posture.

WITHDRAWAL

Excessive withdrawal is more alarming from the point of view of mental health than is the disorderly overaggressiveness of the typical chronic offender. Daydreaming, timidity, and shyness are not in themselves bad. Imaginative boys and girls profit from time to think their own thoughts and to dream out their own ideas. The youngster who withdraws from a group to read may do so just because he finds reading a lot more fun and a lot more stimulating than the conversation of his contemporaries. Generally speaking, you only need to encourage such youngsters to share the activities of their classmates. But withdrawal is a serious symptom in the case of the boy or girl who lives with other children but is always apart from them, who ignores advances, and who daydreams through a lively class discussion.

Investigators studying schizophrenic patients have found that teachers who had them in class but a few years before often fail to remember them. Sometimes they fail even to recognize an individual from his picture, and refuse to believe they could have known him. When the teachers do remember someone of this type, they describe him in phrases like, "He was a boy you couldn't reach," "He was quiet, polite, and bored," "He was just there. He didn't do his work, he just sat and daydreamed."

Sometimes a pupil will be withdrawn one day and overaggressive the next. Such periodic swings in mood from one extreme to another are also a bad sign. In a case history of a boy who was being referred to a psychiatric clinic, a teacher writes: "He tends to fall off into a dream world. It's as though he were lost in a personal fog. When I call his name, he has difficulty in struggling back and picking up contact with what is going on. But on some days, especially on the playground, he will push, punch, and knock down girls. He seems deliberate in his attacks on them, to be acting out of spite. But even on these days he is most often quiet in the classroom---not a discipline problem."

That withdrawing children do not participate actively in the work of the class and are not discipline problems probably explains why teachers so often fail to notice and remember them. But if you are aware of withdrawal as a symptom of maladjustment and of potential mental illness, you will be as eager to give the quiet child personal attention as you are to take the time necessary to help his more obstreperous classmate.

You must move slowly and carefully in your attempts to induce the quiet youngster to take a more active part in work and play with other children. If you suddenly push him into the limelight, he may suffer so acutely that he will immediately withdraw still further into himself. Include him in small groups. Ask him questions that you are sure he can answer, and that can be answered briefly. Give him inconspicuous roles in plays. When he does a good piece of work, mention the fact, but group his name with the names of others whom you are praising. If he shows signs of coming out of his shell, increase your demands on him gradually and let him have some intervals when you leave participation to his own initiative. If over a period of time his tendency to withdraw does not decrease, do your best to arrange to have the child given an individual psychological examination, preferably at a child-guidance clinic that has a psychiatrist on its staff.

One teacher writes:

Nancy was one of the shyest children I've ever seen in all my years of teaching the sixth grade. At the beginning of the year she never took any part in class. If I spoke to her, she "froze" like a frightened rabbit. I investigated and found that her mother had recently been committed to the state hospital for the mentally ill. The school doctor examined Nancy and said that he feared she might be a case of incipient schizophrenia. He arranged to have her treated at the city mental-hygiene clinic. The psychiatric social worker from the clinic helped me make plans to bolster Nancy's self-confidence little by little. Throughout the winter, Nancy went to the clinic regularly. By the following May, she was a different child. The change had been so gradual that I was not really aware of it until one day on the playground I heard the teacher she had had the previous year say with surprise, "Why, there is Nancy, playing kick-ball with the gang. Why, she's just like the others."

A SUMMARY OF CONSTRUCTIVE ACTIONS

As you plan concentrated effort to help a pupil whom you consider maladjusted, you will want to have in mind the procedures you can ethically carry out by yourself or with the aid of the ordinary resources of your school. Here is a brief summary of recommendations from the previous chapters.

Establish rapport. The pupil should feel that you are a friend to whom he can talk freely and upon whom he can depend in time of trouble and all the time. Since he may take you as a model, set a good example.

Compile a case history. Information about a pupil's background is your guide to the causes of his difficulties. Information about his abilities, interests, and plans is your guide to action.

Supply all emotional needs in full measure. If you employ the shotgun attack, you may conquer a maladjustment whose cause you would never be able to discover.

Inspire worthy goals. A goal that is important to the individual leads him to try to do his best and, by centering his thoughts and actions on a definite objective, integrates his personality. A famous psychiatrist always begins his treatment by asking the patient, "Why do you want to get well?"

Enlist the cooperation of the class. The maladjusted child particularly needs to feel that he is a member of the group. If you approach his peers wisely, they think of many ways to help him. And in the process they will learn a valuable lesson in human relations.

Consider physical needs and handicaps. There is always a possibility that some illness, injury, or defect is causing or complicating maladjustment. Read the health records, secure a thorough physical examination for the pupil, and get the advice and the help of the nurse and doctor.

Adjust the curriculum and methods of instruction to the abilities and interests of the individual. One frequent and serious aggravation of maladjustment is the frustration from which the scholastic misfit suffers when he is asked to do academic work in which he is sure to fail. On the other hand, do not forget that the very bright pupil who is not challenged to use his abilities to the full may deteriorate into a lazy daydreamer.

Work with parents. The home remains the major influence on the adjustment and behavior of the child. Your professional training qualifies you to advise parents about matters of child development, including children's emotional needs, and about discipline.

Work with community and public agencies devoted to the care and supervision of children. Social agencies, clinics, the courts, the police, and recreation agencies offer services that are not usually available from within the school system. Children and their parents often need expert help, which you are not qualified to give.

HELP FROM PSYCHOLOGISTS AND PSYCHIATRISTS

You will frequently wish that you could have the help of an expert when you are working with a maladjusted pupil. Unfortunately, there is a great shortage of both psychologists and psychiatrists in the United States. It has been estimated that there is employment available for 15,000 school psychologists and that only a few hundred are actually employed. The number of psychiatrists is not keeping pace with the increase in population. Psychiatrists in practice are mainly employed in hospitals for the mentally ill or in private practice in large cities. Practically no public school has a full-time psychiatrist on its staff. In some states, there are no psychiatrists who specialize in the treatment of children.

If you work in a school that does not have a well-established system for referring pupils for psychological and psychiatric examinations, try to discover what resources are available in your neighborhood and state. The school doctor and your own family doctor will have had experience in certifying mental patients for admission to hospitals and may be able to give you the names and addresses of psychiatrists and of child-guidance clinics. Your state department of education or the state department of health may publish a list. The National Association for Mental Health (10 Columbus Circle, New York 19, N.Y.) and your state association for mental health stand ready to help. But someone who is convinced of the urgency of securing proper care for maladjusted children must take the initiative.

If you are able to secure psychological or psychiatric service for a pupil, it is important that you know what to expect. Experience shows that teachers and parents who refer a child to a clinic expect an immediate disappearance of the difficulty. They forget that the causes of the trouble have probably been operating for a long time and are now deep seated, and that any change for the better will probably be slow and there may be setbacks from time to time.

Psychology, broadly defined, is the science of behavior. The fully qualified psychologist holds the Ph.D. or Ed.D. degree and has served an internship in a specialty, such as school psychology, guidance, or clinical psychology. With less preparation, a person can work in the field of psychology as a psychometrician or a psychological assistant.

The psychologist is able to give you a good estimate of a pupil's intellectual level, of his various abilities, and of his achievement. He may corroborate your judgment, or he may discover that part of the pupil's trouble is due to the fact that he is less—or more—able than you had thought when you were determining what demands to make upon him. The psychologist can also tell you whether or not the pupil is working up to his ability, and even when he is overworking in the attempt to attain a goal that is beyond his native power. The psychologist, by determining a pupil's ability and achievement, can make recommendations regarding grade placement, and particularly regarding the desirability of moving a pupil ahead. He may use special techniques to explore a pupil's interests and discover some with which you can coordinate schoolwork and thus improve motivation. The psychologist's study of the special abilities and disabilities of older boys and girls enables him to suggest desirable educational and vocational plans for them. He can at least make it clear to a youngster when a proposed career is out of line in any direction. The school psychologist, out of his special knowledge and out of his experience with schools, may be able to give you some practical suggestions for handling a pupil in the classroom. If he has the clinical knowledge and experience necessary, he may be able to give you an insight into the pupil's personal problems so that you will understand why he behaves as he does and what he most needs from you, from his studies, and from his classmates. The qualified psychologist may also work directly with individual pupils to help them solve their problems, personal, educational, and vocational.

A psychiatrist is a doctor of medicine who specializes in the treatment of people who are maladjusted and mentally ill. The psychiatrist's training gives him a special knowledge of the basic causes of personality difficulties and of means of discovering and correcting them. He can help you understand a pupil's behavior and needs. However, he will probably be most concerned in working directly with the pupil and the pupil's parents. If the psychiatrist works at a clinic, the clinic's staff will probably include a psychiatric social worker, who will confer with you and with the pupil's parents and see that plans for helping the child are coordinated.

In some schools a psychiatrist works as a consultant to the teachers rather than directly with individual pupils. Dr. I. N. Berlin has described his experience in this capacity (Mental Hygiene, Vol. XL, No. 2, April, 1956). He found that the best method was to have the teacher, the principal, and the school nurse gather all possible information on the family history and early life of the child. This information helped create an understanding of the child's behavior and the origins of his difficulties in his preschool experiences. Often the sympathy and understanding that the teacher acquired was immediately helpful to the child. In discussing seriously disturbed children, the psychiatrist illustrated from his own experience the fact that treatment is necessarily difficult, that it usually takes a long time to see any appreciable change in the child even when work is carried on with the parents at the same time, and that sometimes the best efforts of a team at a clinic fail. Moreover, the psychiatrist pointed out that a difficult child often made him feel angry and frustrated, but that when he permitted himself these feelings and discussed them with others, he felt more at ease with himself and the child. The teachers were relieved to know that "maybe they didn't need to love all their pupils." They discovered that if they accepted their own feelings they could accept the child's, and that disturbed children want "an adult who can understand and tolerate the verbal expression of hostile feelings but who can and will prevent, or at least halt, the impulsive, aggressive behavior." Thus encouraged, the teachers became increasingly firm and consistent, and "they felt better, the children felt better, and [there was] more learning in a more agreeable class atmosphere." Dr. Berlin became convinced that, "if I could be of some help in reducing the anxiety, tensions, and self-doubts of teachers and administrators, they could do their jobs better. I slowly learned that little, if any, direct advice on the handling of a problem was necessary or helpful. I found that I could not advise a teacher on how to teach better. I could only reduce her tensions which served as obstacles to her teaching...."

Dr. Jack R. Ewalt, Commissioner of the Massachusetts Department of Mental Health, has described how psychologists, psychiatrists, and other professional personnel improve community mental health by working with parents and teachers (in School Psychologists at Mid-Century, edited by Norma E. Cutts, The American Psychological Association, Washington, 1955). The goal is to develop a "feeling for, and skill in handling, the emotional interplay between children, between children and teachers, and among the school faculty. As mothers learn these things through discussing the problems of their own child, as teachers learn through handling the problems of their students, there is gradually built into the community a general use of mental-health principles that are a part of daily living."

THE TEACHER'S OWN MENTAL HEALTH

Your own mental health and adjustment are major factors in the mental health and adjustment of your pupils. And, as we have tried to make clear, good mental health is not a mysterious state of being that one achieves—or fails to achieve—automatically. If you make a conscious effort to practice good mental hygiene, you will be a happier human being, a better member of your family, and most certainly a better teacher. You need not be introspective about this, and you certainly need not worry about it. But common sense dictates an occasional checkup on how you are managing your life.

TEN RULES OF MENTAL HYGIENE

1. Be sure you like your job. Be good at it.

2. Develop interests and hobbies to enjoy in your free time. Plan your life to have plenty of recreation and change.

3. Keep in the best physical health. Consult your family doctor if you feel ill or cannot keep from worrying. If he recommends that you see a psychiatrist, accept his advice as calmly and readily as you would if he were recommending any other specialist.

4. Seek friends you enjoy, and maintain the friendships. Meet your friends more than halfway.

5. Do things for people who need assistance—not just out of duty or charity, but because you want to give them help and

pleasure. Try to help and please others when you are most disturbed yourself.

6. Enjoy the beauty and humor that come your way, and, if you do not see them, keep searching for them.

7. Exercise your sense of humor by laughing with your friends and at yourself.

8. Cultivate some activity in addition to your job that you like and can do well, to be sure that you have your share of success.

9. Develop the ability to rely on yourself to make decisions after reasonable consideration and to assume responsibility that is rightly yours.

10. Face reality squarely and courageously. Work out the best solution you can find to your problems.

POINTS TO REMEMBER

Mental health is the world's Number One health problem.

Your work as a teacher gives you the opportunity to play an important role in the prevention of mental illness and so in the future welfare and happiness of many of your pupils.

Any behavior that is unusual for a child of a given age or is unusually frequent, intense, or prolonged may be a symptom of maladjustment. Be particularly alert to discover the quiet, withdrawing child who never calls attention to himself. Unusual quietness is an unfavorable symptom.

When you have a maladjusted pupil, consider carefully all the possible ways in which you might help him, and employ as many of these as you can.

Know the resources of your school system, community, and state for helping maladjusted children. Be quick to call on whatever expert assistance you can command.

Practice the three R's of mental hygiene, Recreation, Routine, and Rest, and don't forget the three S's, Self-esteem, Success, and Security.

Books and Pamphlets to Read

Emotional Adjustment—A Key to Good Citizenship. Detroit Public Schools and Wayne University, Wayne University Press, Detroit, 1953.

Fostering Mental Health in Our Schools. Association for Supervision and Curriculum Adjustment, National Education Association, Washington, 1950.

It Takes All Kinds, by Paul Yaffee. Metropolitan School Study Council, New York, 1955.

Mental Health in Education, by Henry Clay Lindgren. Henry Holt and Company, Inc., New York, 1954.

Topics for Study and Research

Detailed studies of the school behavior of individuals who have become mentally ill. Because relatively few maladjusted people enter mental hospitals before they are 20 years old, much of our knowledge of their school behavior is based on admittedly vague memories. If cumulative records were preserved for ten or more years, they might yield information that would assist teachers in recognizing the early symptoms of maladjustment.

School and Community Projects

School and community child-guidance services: psychological, psychiatric, and social.

A local branch of the National Association for Mental Health.

PTA Meeting

Films: Mental Illness. Encyclopaedia Britannica Films, Wilmette, Ill. Shyness. McGraw-Hill Book Company. Text-Film Department, 330 West 42nd St., New York 36, N. Y.

Topic: The prevention of mental illness.

INDEX

AAA Safety Patrol, 23
abilities, 15-16, 45-46, 47
  see also intelligence
ability grouping, 71-72, 146, 148
  see also special class
acceleration, 70-72
accidents, 33
achievement, 47, 68-69, 160
acne, 52
administration, role of, 7-8, 148-49
  see also principal
adolescence, 129-51
adopted children, 105-7
affection, 43, 116, 121
  see also love
age: mental, 66-67
  range in grade, 70-71
  verification of, 66
aggression: aftereffect of illness, 51
  compulsive, 6, 51
  control of, 41, 57, 161
  and frustration, 65
  and maladjustment, 153, 156
  in teen-agers, 135
  see also fighting
Ames, Louise B., 89, 90
antagonism, 38-39
anxiety, teacher's feelings of, 9
arbitrariness, 12
arson, 117
assault, 35, 117, 118, 126
assembly, disorder in, 137
asthma, 52
attention-seeking, 13, 18, 66, 82
automobile driving, 134, 145-46, 148

Berlin, I. N., 161
big brother, teacher as, 125

Birch, Jack W., 73
boredom, 65-66
bossiness, 82
  see also domination
bowel control, 51-52, 87
boys: behavior of, 2, 31, 113, 118, 131
  development of, 132-33
brain injury, 51, 54, 57-58
Brandwein, Paul F., 73
Bronner, Augusta, 112, 116
building, inadequate, 7
bullying, 52

case history, 46-47, 124, 158, 161-62
changing seat, 32, 41-42
cheating, 131
chores, classroom, 76, 103
  see also responsibility
chronic offenders, defined, 2
Church, Richard, 52-53
class: attitude of, 2, 44-45
  cooperation of, 158
  management of, 6-25
  size of, 131
classroom: arrangement of, 10-11
  emotional tone of, 6
  lighting, temperature, ventilation of, 10, 17
clowning, 82
comic books, 115
community agencies, work with, 61, 93-94, 159
  see also social worker
Community Chest, 94
community council, 145
compulsive behavior, 51
conferences: case, 93-94
  with class, 12-13, 21, 23, 142

165